The BIG GEORGIA

REPRODUCIBLE

Activity Book!

BY CAROLE MARSH

This activity book has material which correlates with
the Georgia Quality Core Curriculum.

At every opportunity, we have tried to relate information to
the History and Social Science, English, Science, Math, Civics,
Economics, and Computer Technology QCC directives.

For additional information, go to our websites:
www.georgiaexperience.com or **www.gallopade.com**.

The Big Activity Book Team

Billie Walburn

Michael Marsh

Debra Sims

Michele Yother

Carole Marsh

Bob Longmeyer

William Nesbitt, Jr.

Kathy Zimmer

Jill Sanders

Cranston Davenport

Steven Saint-Laurent

Sue Gentzke

Sherry Moss

Cecil Anderson

Chad Beard

Jennifer McGann

Karin Peterson

Wanda Coats

Gallopade is proud to be a member of these educational organizations and associations:

Published by

GALLOPADE™
INTERNATIONAL

800-536-2GET
www.gallopade.com

SHOPA MEMBER™
School, Home, & Office Products Association

NSSEA

The Georgia Experience Series

The Georgia Experience! Paperback Book

My First Pocket Guide to Georgia!

The Big Georgia Reproducible Activity Book!

The Peachy Georgia Coloring Book!

My First Book About Georgia!

Georgia Jeopardy: Answers & Questions About Our State

Georgia "Jography!": A Fun Run Through Our State

The Georgia Experience! Sticker Pack

The Georgia Experience! Poster/Map

Discover Georgia CD-ROM

Georgia "GEO" Bingo Game

Georgia "HISTO" Bingo Game

A Word From The Author

Georgia is a very special state. Almost everything about Georgia is interesting and fun! It has a remarkable history that helped create the great nation of America. Georgia enjoys an amazing geography of incredible beauty and fascination. The state's people are unique and have accomplished many great things.

This Activity Book is chockful of activities to entice you to learn more about Georgia. While completing mazes, dot-to-dots, word searches, coloring activities, word codes, and other fun-to-do activities, you'll learn about Georgia's history, geography, people, places, animals, legends, and more.

Whether you're sitting in a classroom, stuck inside on a rainy day, or—better yet—sitting in the back seat of a car touring the wonderful state of Georgia, my hope is that you have as much fun using this Activity Book as I did writing it.

Enjoy your Georgia Experience—it's the trip of a lifetime!!

Carole Marsh

Ya'll Come!

Color the state of Georgia. What color? PEACH, of course! Then, circle the capital city.

• ROME

• ATHENS

☆ ATLANTA

• AUGUSTA

• MACON

• COLUMBUS

SAVANNAH •

• ALBANY

• VALDOSTA

Atlantic Ocean

Columbus Comes to the New World

Christopher Columbus was a famous explorer who sailed across the ocean in 1492 and discovered the New World which we now call America.

Help build a ship for Christopher Columbus.

Draw lines to complete the dot-to-dot. Color the picture.

♪♫♪ Georgia State Song ♫♪♫

"Georgia on my Mind"

Words by Stuart Gorrell, Music by Hoagy Carmichael

Melodies bring memories
That linger in my heart
Make me think of Georgia
Why did we ever part?

Some sweet day, when blossoms fall
And all the world's a song
I'll go back to Georgia
'Cause that's where I belong.

Georgia, Georgia, the whole day through
Just an old sweet song keeps Georgia on my mind.
Georgia, Georgia, a song of you
Comes as sweet and clear as moonlight through the pines.

Other arms reach out to me
Other eyes smile tenderly
Still in peaceful dreams I see
The road leads back to you.

Georgia, Georgia, no peace I find
Just an old sweet song keeps Georgia on my mind.

"Georgia on my Mind" became the "official" state song in 1979!

The lyricist (Stuart Gorrell) wrote about missing his Georgia home. Now, it's *your* turn to be a song writer! Think about a place you've been and write a neat verse about it. Maybe you'll go back to that special place sometime!

_____

_____

_____

_____

_____

_____

_____

Famous Georgia People Scavenger Hunt

Here is a list of some of the famous people from our state. Go on a scavenger hunt to see if you can "capture" a fact about each one. Use an encyclopedia, almanac, or other resource you might need. Happy hunting!

FAMOUS PERSON

Conrad Potter Aiken
Martha Berry
Julian Bond
Jim Brown
Jimmy Carter
Ray Charles
Ty Cobb
Rebecca Latimer Felton
Henry W. Grady
Lewis Grizzard
Button Gwinnett
Lyman Hall
Alonzo Herndon
Maynard H. Jackson
Martin Luther King, Jr.
Crawford W. Long
Juliette Gordon Low
Edward O. Martin
Jessye Norman
John S. Pemberton
Jackie Robinson
Sequoyah
Tomochichi
George Walton
Eli Whitney
Robert Woodruff

FAMOUS FACT

_____
_____
_____
_____
_____
_____
_____
_____
_____
_____
_____
_____
_____
_____
_____
_____
_____
_____
_____
_____
_____
_____
_____
_____
_____
_____

Georgia State Flag

The Georgia state flag is blue with red triangles and white stars. The background of the state seal is white. **Color Georgia's state flag.**

In the Beginning... Came a Colony

In 1732, James Oglethorpe and 35 families sailed from England on the *Anne* in search of the new British colony of Georgia. In 1733, they landed at Yamacraw Bluff and rowed up the Savannah River, where they met a group of Yamacraw Indians. Chief Tomochichi said it would be OK for the settlers to stay. They pitched their tents and started the city of Savannah—the first "planned" city in the United States.

Help the *Anne* sail across the Atlantic Ocean to Savannah.

Savannah

Finish

Start

England

Our State Bird!

Connect the dots to see Georgia's beautiful state bird, the Brown Thrasher.

When you are done, color the bird.

Write the bird's name in the space below.

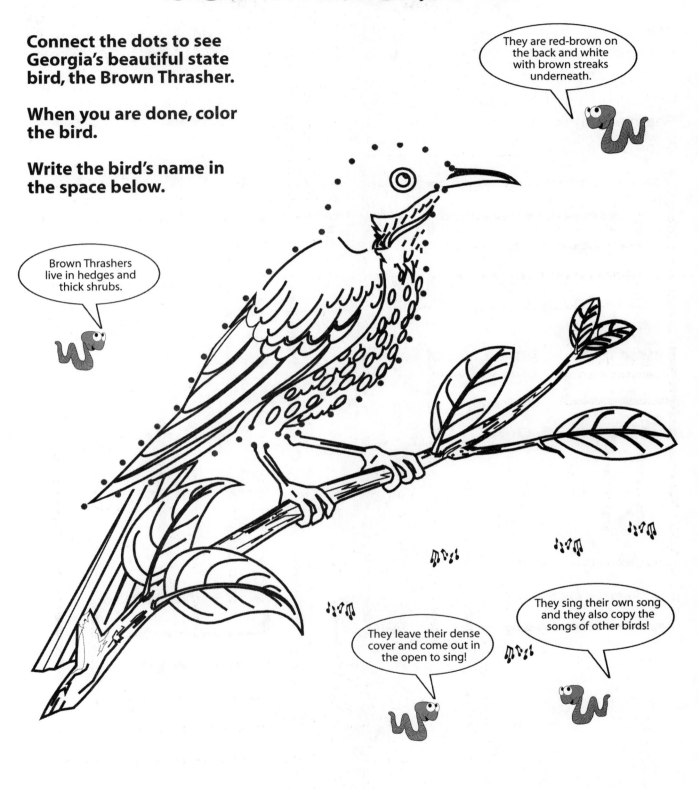

They are red-brown on the back and white with brown streaks underneath.

Brown Thrashers live in hedges and thick shrubs.

They leave their dense cover and come out in the open to sing!

They sing their own song and they also copy the songs of other birds!

_____ _____

Buzzing Around Georgia!

Write the answers to the questions below. Follow a path through the maze in the same order as your answers to get the bee to the beehive.

Georgia is bordered by the _____ Ocean.

Georgia is one of the original _____ states.

Georgia is in _____ America.

American _____ were the first people to live in Georgia.

The _____ River is in the northern mountains region.

Georgia has a sandy region called the Coastal _____.

The capital of Georgia is _____.

One of Georgia's nicknames is the _____ State.

Georgia was founded by Englishman, James _____.

America's first "planned" city is _____.

The number one crop grown in Georgia is _____.

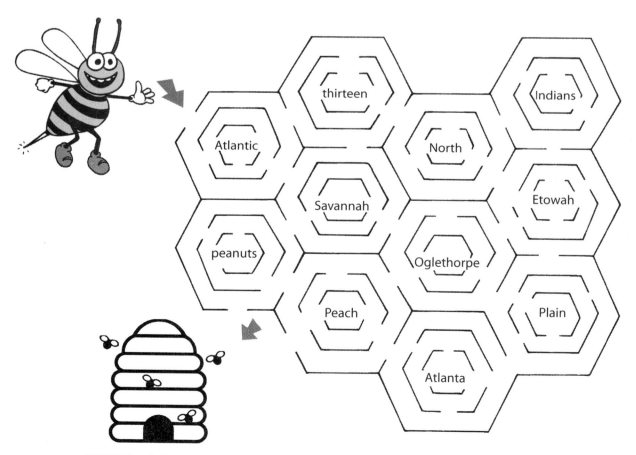

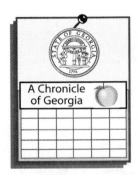

A Chronicle of Georgia

Georgia Through the Years

Many great things have happened in Georgia throughout its history, both past and present. Chronicle the following important Georgia events by solving math problems to find out the years in which they happened.

1. Spanish expedition led by Hernando de Soto enters Georgia. 2-1=   2+3=   2+2=   1-1=

2. King George II of England grants charter for colony of Georgia. 6-5=   1+6=   2+1=   1+1=

3. James Oglethorpe and British settlers arrive and establish Savannah. 5-4=   3+4=   6-3=   9/3=

4. Slave trade allowed in Georgia. 7-6=   6+1=   9-4=   2-2=

5. Revolutionary War begins. 9-8=   8-1=   5+2=   2+3=

6. Declaration of Independence signed. 3-2=   1x7=   3+4=   8-2=

7. Georgia becomes 4th state to ratify the United States Constitution. 8-7=   9-2=   2x4=   4x2=

8. Cherokee Indians forced to leave Georgia on tragic "Trail of Tears." 6-5=   3+5=   9/3=   9-1=

9. Georgia secedes from Union. 4-3=   4+4=   5+1=   6-5=

10. Civil War ends, slavery is abolished, and secession is repealed. 1+0=   9-1=   1+5=   5/1=

11. Georgia is readmitted to the Union. 9/9=   6+2=   2+5=   9-9=

12. New state constitution is adopted. 5-4=   8-0=   9-2=   8-1=

13. Federal District Court orders racially balanced schools. 3/3=   7+2=   6/1=   9/1=

14. Georgia hosts the Summer Olympics. 6-5=   2+7=   1+8=   3+3=

ANSWERS: 1-1540; 2-1732; 3-1733; 4-1750; 5-1775; 6-1776; 7-1788; 8-1838; 9-1861; 10-1865; 11-1870; 12-1877; 13-1969; 14-1996

Rhymin' Riddles

I am a state on the East Coast and my name starts with a "G";
A lot of my historic sites many tourists come to see.

What am I? _____

I lived in Georgia before the colonists did come;
On the lands near rivers and streams were my tribe's home.

Who am I? _____

The Declaration of Independence was signed by me;
Georgia's tenth governor I then turned out to be.

Who am I? _____ _____

With my soldiers, Florida and Georgia I did explore;
Land of the New World so Spain could have more.

Who am I? _____ _____ _____

On the Georgia–Florida border I sprawl;
Within my murky waters many snakes and critters do crawl.

What am I? _____ _____

ANSWERS: Georgia; Indians; Lyman Hall; Hernando de Soto; Okefenokee Swamp

All Around
Georgia!
Crossword Puzzle

Georgia is surrounded by five states and one body of water. To find out what they are, fill in the crossword using the clues below.

1. **A state north of Georgia** (across)
2. **A body of water east of Georgia** (down)
3. **A state south of Georgia** (across)
4. **A state northeast of Georgia** (across)
5. **Another state northeast of Georgia** (across)
6. **A state west of Georgia** (down)

Compass
Rose

ANSWERS: 1-Tennessee; 2-Atlantic Ocean; 3-Florida; 4-South Carolina; 5-North Carolina; 6-Alabama

Food Festivals!

Do you have a favorite food? Georgia has a festival to satisfy all of your taste buds.

Draw a line from each festival to the food that goes with it.

- Cornelia's Big Red Apple Festival

- Georgia Peach Festival in Fort Valley

- Lake Lanier Islands' Great Pumpkin Festival

- Big Pig Jig (Barbeque Cooking Contest) in Vienna

- Sea Island Festival at Neptune Park on St. Simons Island

- Plains Peanut Festival

Sing Like a Georgia Bird
Word Jumble

Arrange the jumbled letters in the proper order for the names of birds found in Georgia.

BLUE JAY

CARDINAL

CROW

FINCH

BROWN THRASHER

ORIOLE

ROBIN

SPARROW

WARBLER

WOODPECKER

N I D L A R A C _ _ _ _ _ _ _ _

O O I R L E _ _ _ _ _ _

N I B O R _ _ _ _ _

H C N I F _ _ _ _ _

R O W C _ _ _ _

S P R R W O A _ _ _ _ _ _ _

B E U L   A J Y _ _ _ _   _ _ _

B R L W A R E _ _ _ _ _ _ _

N W O R B   R E H S A R H T _ _ _ _ _   _ _ _ _ _ _ _

D O O W P C E E K R _ _ _ _ _ _ _ _ _

Surgery Without Pain!

Crawford W. Long, a Georgia surgeon, was concerned about his patients and the pain they felt during surgery. He had a patient who needed to have two tumors removed from his neck. The patient, James Venable, would not agree to surgery because he dreaded the pain *(who wouldn't?)*. Dr. Long thought about using an anesthetic, a substance to numb the part of the body needing surgery or put the patient to sleep during the operation.

Mr. Venable agreed to try the new procedure. On May 30, 1842, Dr. Long performed the first "pain-free" and successful operation using the new anesthetic!

To discover the name of the new anesthetic and complete the sentence below, circle the even number letters and list them below:

In 1842, Dr. Crawford W. Long became the first surgeon to operate using

— .

1 L	2 E	3 I	4 T	5 N	6 H	7 C
8 E	9 Z	10 R	11 N	12 A	13 J	14 S
15 F	16 T	17 P	18 H	19 S	20 E	21 T
22 A	23 H	24 N	25 W	26 E	27 P	28 S
29 R	30 T	31 E	32 H	33 S	34 E	35 I
36 T	37 O	38 I	39 A	40 C	41 S	42 !

ANSWER: Ether as the anesthetic!

Let's Get Regional!

Georgia is divided into three major regions. The Blue Ridge Mountains, part of the Appalachian range, are in northern Georgia. The Piedmont Plateau, the most densely populated region, lies between the mountains and the Coastal Plain. The Fall Line Hills separate the Piedmont Plateau from the Coastal Plain. The Coastal Plain, the largest of the regions, makes up the southern part of the state and meets the Atlantic Ocean.

Map Key!

A map key is a list of the symbols on a map. Symbols are pictures that stand for something real.

Draw these symbols on the map.

Mountains

Coastal Plain

Piedmont Plateau

Color the map as follows:

Coastal Plain-yellow
Piedmont Plateau-green
Mountains-blue

Early Georgia Abounds with Mounds!

As early as 8000 B.C., Mound Builders inhabited Georgia. Beside rivers and streams, they built pyramids flattened at the top that were as high as 60 feet (18 meters). These pyramids were made of dirt or piled shells and sometimes in the form of rings or circles. For centuries, tribal towns flourished in the shadows of these man-made hills.

You can still see some of these mounds today, including Etowah Mounds near Cartersville, Ocmulgee National Monument near Macon, and Kolomoki Mounds in southwestern Georgia.

As early as 1000 A.D. Cherokee Indians, who lived in hillside dwellings, came to Georgia from the north. Creek Indians, who often lived beside streams, moved in from the southwest, conquering the Mound Builders they encountered.

See if you can match their smarts by completing the matching below!

1. 1000 A.D.

2. Creek Indians

3. They traveled on foot because they had no …

4. Mounds

5. Crops grown

6. Etowah Mounds near Cartersville

7. Beside rivers and streams

8. 8000 B.C.

A. Mound Builders inhabited Georgia

B. corn and squash

C. conquered the Mound Builders they encountered when they came to Georgia from the southwest

D. you can still see these mounds today

E. where Creek Indians camped

F. horses

G. Cherokee Indians came to Georgia

H. flat topped pyramids as high as 60 feet (18 meters)

> Would you like to work on an archaeological dig?

ANSWERS: 1-G; 2-C; 3-F; 4-H; 5-B; 6-D; 7-E; 8-A

Who Am I?

★★★   ★★★

I ...

... *was one of the most famous generals in the Civil War.*

... *was very loyal, but my side, the Confederacy, lost the Civil War.*

... *surrendered at Appomattox Court House to Union General Ulysses S. Grant.*

Draw lines to complete the dot-to-dot.

Color my picture.

In 1861, Georgia became the fifth state to leave the Union and join ten other states in the Confederacy.

Finish 47.
Start 1.

WHO AM I?

_____ ___ _____

ANSWER: Robert E. Lee

©2000 Carole Marsh/Gallopade International/800-536-2GET/www.georgiaexperience.com/Page 21

Beautiful Butterfly!

Using the key, color the picture of Georgia's State Butterfly.

COLOR KEY:

1. black   2. yellow   3. red   4. blue   5. gray

Can you guess the name of this lovely insect?

_____ _____ Butterfly

Make a Wampum Necklace!

Georgia Indians used wampum (beads made from colored shells) to barter with early settlers. They traded wampum for food and supplies. The Indians sometimes traded wampum for trinkets.

You can make your own wampum necklace using dried macaroni and string. Thread the dried macaroni onto a long piece of string and tie.

Wear your necklace to show your pride in your Georgia ancestors!

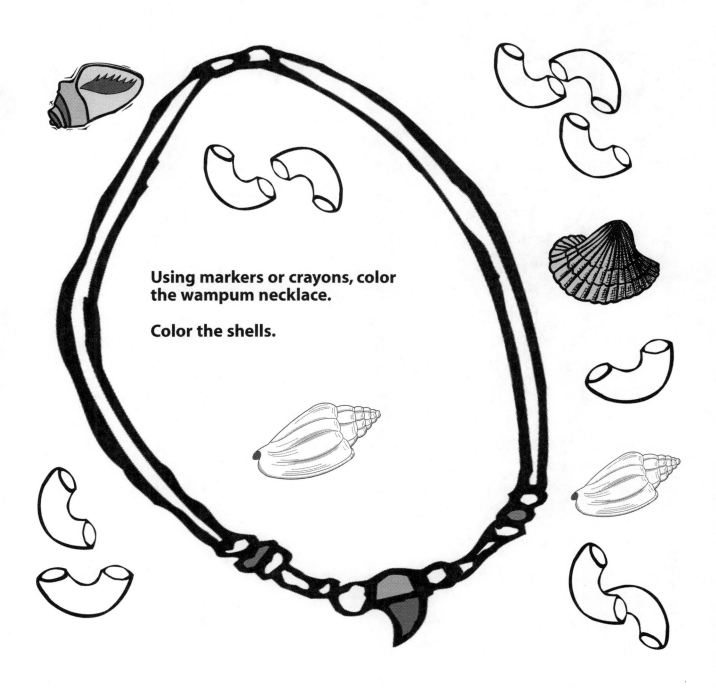

Using markers or crayons, color the wampum necklace.

Color the shells.

A Cherokee Princess and a Chickasaw Brave!

In the north Georgia Mountains, a sad tale of unrequited love unfolds...Sautee was a Chickasaw brave and Nacoochee was a Cherokee Indian princess. Their two tribes were at war, so the couple were not supposed to be together. They loved each other so much, they were willing to do anything—so they ran off together.

They came back to plead for peace between the two tribes. Nacoochee's father had Sautee thrown from a cliff to his death. Nacoochee, not able to live without her love, jumped off the cliff to be with him forever.

Grief-stricken, Nacoochee's father realized how much they loved each other and buried them together in the mound you'll find outside of the north Georgia mountain town of Helen.

A *legend* is a story that cannot be proven to be based on history or the truth. It is handed down through tradition.

Now it's your turn to write a legend:

_____

_____

_____

_____

_____

Frankly, My Dear!

Plantation life during the Antebellum period (pre-Civil War) South changed dramatically after the war. Former slaves now required wages for their work, but plantation owners did not have the money to pay them. As a result, tenant farming was born. Plantation owners rented out parts of their land to poor farmers, both black and white. As payment for renting the land, the new tenants agreed to give a share of their crops to the owners at the end of the growing season.

Color the Southern Belle and her plantation.

Margaret Mitchell's famous Civil War novel, *Gone With the Wind*, tells the story of the O'Hara family and their beloved Tara Plantation in Clayton County near Atlanta. It's the best-selling novel of all time and has been translated into 36 languages. That's a lot of different ways to say, "Frankly, My Dear!"

Thar's Gold in Them Thar Hills!

In 1540, Hernando de Soto of Spain led the first European explorers into Georgia. De Soto and the Spanish Conquistadors were looking for cities of gold and Native Americans to convert to Christianity. His expedition recorded North America's first Christian baptism near Ocmulgee, but they never found any gold.

De Soto arrived a couple of hundred years too early. In 1828, gold was discovered in Dahlonega in the northeastern mountains of Georgia and started America's first gold rush!

See if you can help this conquistador find the golden treasure!

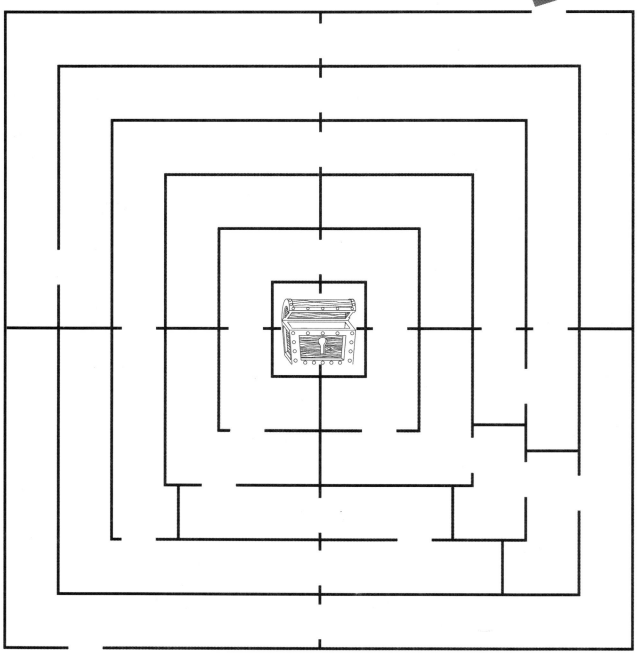

Just Peachy Peach Cobbler

The Peach State is famous for its __ __ __ __ __ __ __ *(peaches, of course!)*. Have you ever had a Peach Cobbler? They're easy to make—here, we'll show you how! Maybe you can get Mom or Dad to help you with this scrumptious recipe:

For the crust, you will need:

1 - cup all-purpose flour   1 - pinch of salt
2 - tablespoons of sugar   1 - stick of butter
1 - tablespoon cold water

Step 1: Blend flour, sugar, salt, and butter with fork
Step 2: Spoon in water and blend with fork.
Step 3: Knead dough 3 or 4 times.
Step 4: Roll out dough and cut into strips.

For the filling, you will need:

3 - cups cooked or canned peaches
2/3 - cup of sugar (that's 2/3 of a cup)

Step 1: Add sugar to the fruit.
Step 2: Heat, but do not boil.

You can double the crust recipe and put a layer on the bottom of the greased pan before you add the fruit....

...after you add the fruit, go ahead and put the strips of dough on top and bake. It'll be twice as crusty and twice as good!

To put it all together:

Step 1: Grease an 8" x 8" pan and put fruit in it.
Step 2: Place strips of dough on top of fruit filling.
Step 3: Poke holes in the top with a knife or fork, dot with butter, and sprinkle with cinnamon
Step 4: Bake in an oven at 400°F for 1/2 hour.
Step 5: When cobbler is done, scoop some into a big bowl and add vanilla ice cream on top.
Step 6: ENJOY!

A Rough Row to Hoe!

The people who first came to Georgia were faced with a lot of hard work to survive in the New World. **Circle the things settlers in Georgia would need.**

A Day in the Life of a Colonist!

**Pretend you were a colonist in the days of early Georgia.
You kept a diary of what you did each day.
Write in the "diary" what you might have done
on a long, hot summer day in July, 1734.**

_____

_____

_____

_____

_____

_____

_____

_____

_____

_____

_____

_____

_____

Georgia, The Peach State!

Match the name of each Georgia state symbol on the left with its picture on the right.

State Fossil

State Vegetable

State Butterfly

State Flower

State Tree

State Fish

State Shell

State Insect

State Bird

Largemouth Bass

Brown Thrasher

Knobbed Whelk

Cherokee Rose

Tiger Swallowtail Butterfly

Vidalia Onion

Live Oak

Shark Tooth

Honeybee

Georgia Writers

Fill in the missing first or last name of these famous Georgia writers.

1. First name: Margaret
   Last name: _____

2. First name: _____
   Last name: Kay

3. First name: Celestine
   Last name: _____

4. First name: _____
   Last name: Price

5. First name: Erskine
   Last name: _____

6. First name: _____
   Last name: Rivers Siddons

7. First name: Olive Ann
   Last name: _____

To read, or not to read? That is the question! There's only one answer... to read!

ANSWERS: 1-Mitchell; 2-Terry; 3-Sibley; 4-Eugenia; 5-Caldwell; 6-Anne; 7-Burns

The First Americans

When European explorers first arrived in America, they found many American Indian tribes living here.

Eastern Woodland Indians lived in the Eastern region of the United States. The types of homes they lived in were wigwams and longhouses. **Color the Eastern Woodland green.**

Plains Indians lived all over the Great Plains region of North America. Some Plains Indians lived in teepees. **Color the Great Plains yellow.**

Pueblo Indians lived in the Southwest region of North America. They lived in multi-story terraced buildings. **Color the Southwest red.**

Color these houses Indians lived in.
Then draw a line from the type of house to the correct region.

An Original State!

Georgia is one of the first 13 states of the United States of America. The original colonists came to Georgia and the other colonies from Western Europe.

Color the 13 original states using the COLOR KEY.

COLOR KEY

Pennsylvania - Orange
Massachusetts - Yellow
North Carolina - Orange
New Hampshire - Red
South Carolina - Yellow
Rhode Island - Green
Connecticut - Blue
New York - Purple
New Jersey - Red
Delaware - Yellow
Maryland - Green
Virginia - Blue
Georgia - Red

circa 1787

New Hampshire
New York
Massachusetts
Rhode Island
Connecticut
Pennsylvania
New Jersey
Ohio River
Delaware
Virginia
Maryland
North Carolina
South Carolina
Georgia

GEORGIA IS ONE OF THE STATES TO BE ON A YEAR-2000 COMMEMORATIVE QUARTER! SEE...!

GEORGIA WAS THE 4TH STATE TO RATIFY THE U.S. CONSTITUTION, BUT...

...GEORGIA WAS THE LAST (13TH) COLONY TO BE SETTLED!

The British are coming!
The British are coming!
And they're looking for a fight!

In 1775, when Georgia was about 40 years old, the Revolutionary War with England started. In March 1776, British warships sailed up the Savannah River looking for supplies. They found Georgia patriots instead. The battle that followed marked Georgia's entry into the Revolutionary War and is known as the Battle of Rice Boats.

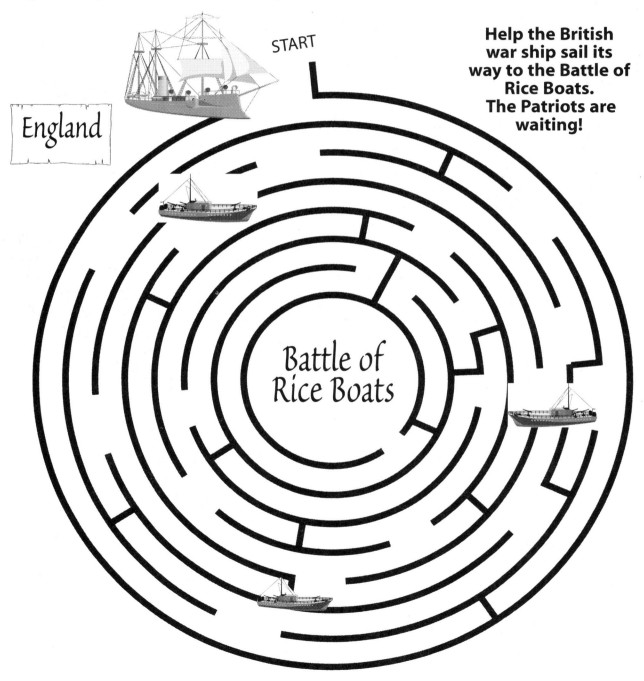

Help the British war ship sail its way to the Battle of Rice Boats. The Patriots are waiting!

START

England

Battle of Rice Boats

Independence Day

We celebrate America's birthday on July 4. We call the 4th of July Independence Day because this is the day America declared its independence from England.

Circle the things you might enjoy on this special holiday.

Georgia had three signers of the Declaration of Independence: Button Gwinnett, Lyman Hall, and George Walton.

Pretend you are signing the Declaration of Independence.

Declaration of Independence

_____

Write your signature here.
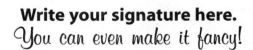

July 1994: Rain, Rain, Go Away! Please!

Unscramble each word in the word bank and fill in the blanks to get all the details on this Georgia disaster.

WORD BANK

(1) **turalna**   (2) **Altober**   (3) **tialtorren**   (4) **Ftlin**

(5) **pageram**   (6) **loodfed**   (7) **kenchics**   (8) **Ablnya**

(9) **finscof**   (10) **fishcat**   (11) **hsif**   (12) **amws**

Georgia experienced its worst (1) __ __ __ __ __ __ __ disaster ever during the summer of '94! Tropical Storm (2) __ __ __ __ __ __ __ blew through and brought (3) __ __ __ __ __ __ __ __ __ __ (very heavy) rains which caused the (4) __ __ __ __ __ River to (5) __ __ __ __ __ __ __ its way through the southwestern part of the state.

The Flint River had not (6) __ __ __ __ __ __ __ since 1925, but this time–look out! It rose 37 feet (11 meters), wiping out everything in its path. In Macon County, 25,000 (7) __ __ __ __ __ __ __ __ drowned. Cleanup crews had to wear masks because the smell was so bad!

In (8) __ __ __ __ __ __, neighborhoods became lakes. The flood waters in the streets carried unearthed (9) __ __ __ __ __ __ __ that bobbed to the surface and eerily floated away!

In Newton, owners of a 300-acre (120 hectare) (10) __ __ __ __ __ __ __ farm could do nothing but watch as their breeding ponds overflowed and their (11) __ __ __ __ simply (12) __ __ __ __ away!

More than 30 people lost their lives as the flood submerged an area the size of Rhode Island and Massachusetts combined!

ANSWERS: natural; Alberto; torrential; Flint; rampage; flooded; chickens; Albany; coffins; catfish; fish; swam

What in the World?

A hemisphere is one-half of a sphere (globe) created by the prime meridian or equator. Every place in the world is in two hemispheres (Northern or Southern and Eastern or Western). The equator is an imaginary line that runs around the world from left to right and divides the globe into the Northern Hemisphere and Southern Hemisphere. Georgia is in the Northern Hemisphere.

The prime meridian is an imaginary line that runs around the world from top to bottom and divides the globe into the Eastern Hemisphere and Western Hemisphere. Georgia is in the Western Hemisphere.

Label the Eastern and Western Hemispheres.

Write PM on the prime meridian.

Color the map.

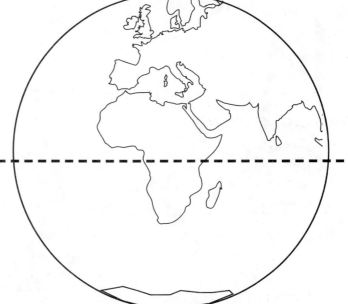

Label the Northern and Southern Hemispheres.

Write E on the equator.

Color the map.

Color Me!

GEORGIA

Brown
Like the Brown Thrasher
Brown

BLUE
Like the sky over Dixie
Blue

YELLOW
Like the Yellow Daisies
Yellow

RED
Like Georgia red clay
Red

Black
BLACK
Like the stripes on a honeybee

Purple
PURPLE
Like the azalea flowers

Green
GREEN
Like the evergreen pine trees

Orange
ORANGE
Like a Georgia sunset

Key to a Map!

A map key, also called a map legend, shows symbols which represent different things on a map.

Match each word with a symbol for things found in the state of Georgia.

Airport

Church

Mountains

Railroad

River

Road

School

State Capital

Battle Site

Bird Sanctuary

What Did They Eateth?
Early American Food Trivia

Below are some foods that Georgians ate long ago. Some are still eaten today—but not named the same!

Match the food with its definition. Check your taste buds, oops - your answers, at the bottom of the page.

1. Succotash
2. Marmalade
3. Fool
4. Shoofly Pie
5. Punch
6. Spoonbread
7. Hoppin' John
8. Salat
9. Apoquinimine cakes
10. Pone
11. Chowder
12. Red-eye gravy
13. Cider
14. Ham Hock

_____ A. Form of beaten biscuits
_____ B. Thick soup made with clams, fish, and vegetables
_____ C. Pan gravy made from fried ham
_____ D. Juice made from apples or other fruit
_____ E. Ankle of a pig
_____ F. Loaf or oval-shaped bread or cake
_____ G. Salad
_____ H. Dish made with black-eyed peas and rice
_____ I. Dish made of corn and beans and salt pork or bacon
_____ J. Baked dish made of cornmeal, eggs, and shortening
_____ K. Jelly or preserves with small pieces of fruit or rind in it
_____ L. English dessert made of crushed, cooked fruit and cream or custard
_____ M. Pie filled with a mixture of flour, butter, brown sugar, and molasses
_____ N. Drink made with two or more fruit juices, sugar, spices, and water

Let's eateth!

Do the time warp back to the present. These are a few of Georgia's famous foods you can enjoy today. How many have you tasted?

Stewed Apples	Black-eyed Peas	Fried Chicken
Sweet Tea	Brunswick Stew	Barbeque
Girl Scout Cookies	Grits with Butter	Fried Catfish
Mashed Potatoes	Vidalia Onions	Peach Cobbler
Boiled Shrimp	Claxton Fruitcake	Roasted Peanuts
Biscuits and Gravy	Fried Green Tomatoes	Pecan Pie

ANSWERS: 1-I; 2-K; 3-L; 4-M; 5-N; 6-J; 7-H; 8-G; 9-A; 10-F; 11-B; 12-C; 13-D; 14-E

ALL AROUND GEORGIA

Georgia is bordered by different states. These states are called neighboring states. We also have an ocean as part of our eastern border. To learn where we are located in the United States, we need to know our neighbors.

On the map below, write the names of our neighboring states, then color them yellow. Name the ocean that borders our state. Color it blue. Color Georgia red.

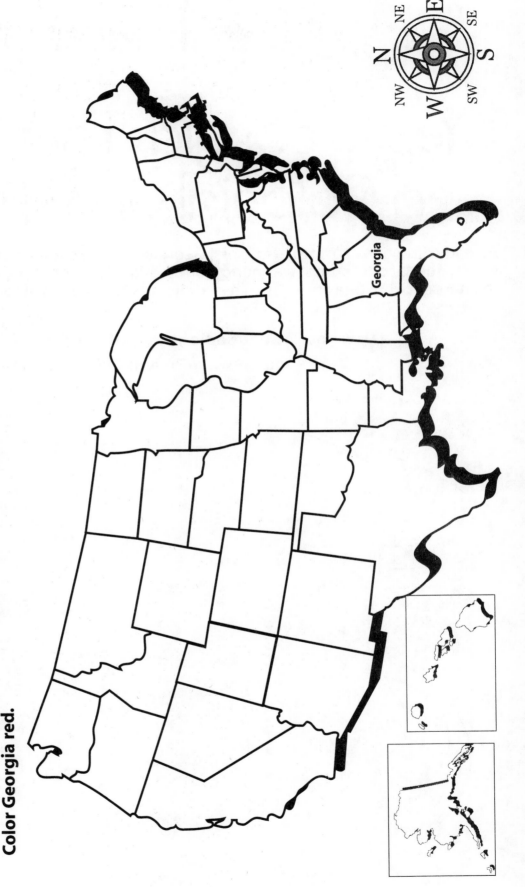

Georgia

Yes, Georgia, There Was a Colonial Christmas!

An early Christmas custom in colonial Georgia was to create a "goodie string" filled with treats. The "goodie string" was hung from the door and each young visitor was allowed to choose a Christmas treat, such as candy, nuts, fruit, or small toys.

Draw your own "goodie string" of Christmas delights.
When you finish, color it in Christmas colors.

Map of North America

This is a map of North America. Georgia is one of the 50 states in North America.

Color the state of Georgia red.

Color the rest of the United States yellow. Alaska and Hawaii are part of the United States and should also be colored yellow.

Color Canada green. Color Mexico blue.

Symbols of the United States

These are some of the symbols that remind us of America. We show these symbols honor and respect.

Color each symbol.

American Flag

Statue of Liberty

Bald Eagle

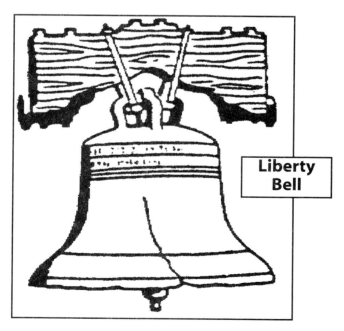
Liberty Bell

$$$$ GEORGIA BANKS $$$$

Georgia banks provide essential financial services.

Some of the services they provide:

*Banks lend money to consumers to purchase goods and services–such as houses, cars, and education.
* Banks lend money to producers who start new businesses.
* Banks issue credit cards.
* Banks provide savings accounts and pay interest to savers.
* Banks provide checking accounts.

You are never too young to start saving $$$$$$$$!

Check whether you would have more, less, or the same amount of money after each event. Then, check your answers!

	MORE	LESS	SAME
1. You deposit your paycheck into your checking account.	MORE	LESS	SAME
2. You put $1,000 in your savings account.	MORE	LESS	SAME
3. You use your credit card to buy new school clothes.	MORE	LESS	SAME
4. You borrow money from the bank to open a toy store.	MORE	LESS	SAME
5. You write a check at the grocery store.	MORE	LESS	SAME
6. You transfer money from checking to savings.	MORE	LESS	SAME

ANSWERS: 1-MORE; 2-MORE; 3-SAME; 4-MORE; 5-LESS; 6-SAME

A River Runs Through It!

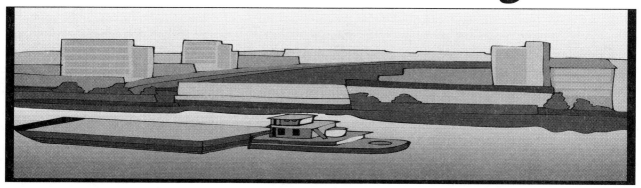

The state of Georgia is blessed with many rivers, lakes, springs, and even a swamp.

Use the chart to discover the rivers below. Come on—wade right in!

A	B	C	D	E	F	G	H	I	J	K	L	M
1	2	3	4	5	6	7	8	9	10	11	12	13

N	O	P	Q	R	S	T	U	V	W	X	Y	Z
14	15	16	17	18	19	20	21	22	23	24	25	26

$\overline{3}$ $\overline{8}$ $\overline{1}$ $\overline{20}$ $\overline{20}$ $\overline{1}$ $\overline{8}$ $\overline{15}$ $\overline{15}$ $\overline{3}$ $\overline{8}$ $\overline{5}$ $\overline{5}$

$\overline{15}$ $\overline{3}$ $\overline{15}$ $\overline{14}$ $\overline{5}$ $\overline{5}$

$\overline{19}$ $\overline{1}$ $\overline{22}$ $\overline{1}$ $\overline{14}$ $\overline{14}$ $\overline{1}$ $\overline{8}$

$\overline{15}$ $\overline{7}$ $\overline{5}$ $\overline{5}$ $\overline{3}$ $\overline{8}$ $\overline{5}$ $\overline{5}$

$\overline{6}$ $\overline{12}$ $\overline{9}$ $\overline{14}$ $\overline{20}$

$\overline{19}$ $\overline{21}$ $\overline{23}$ $\overline{1}$ $\overline{14}$ $\overline{14}$ $\overline{5}$ $\overline{5}$

Did you notice how many Georgia rivers have Native American names?

Plenty of Peach Trees

Georgia is one of the nation's leading producers of peaches. The Peach State is one of Georgia's nicknames. During the last two weeks of March, the landscape is filled with fragrant pink and white blossoms as the peach trees explode with blooms. The official Peach Blossom Trail (U.S. 341 west of I-75) winds from Jonesboro to Perry wiggling its way for 100 miles (160 km) through eight counties that grow 65 percent of Georgia's peaches.

How many trees do you see in the peach orchard below? Write your answer here:

Color the peach trees.

Did you know there are 61 streets in Atlanta that have Peachtree in their name?

For extra fun, count the peaches. Write your answer here:

ANSWERS: 4 trees; 32 peaches

Georgia Battlefields

Many Civil War battles were fought on Georgia's soil. The Civil War ended in 1865 when Confederate General Robert E. Lee surrendered to Union General Ulysses S. Grant at the Appomattox Court House in Virginia.

Draw a line from the name of the location in which each battle occurred to the correct place on the map.

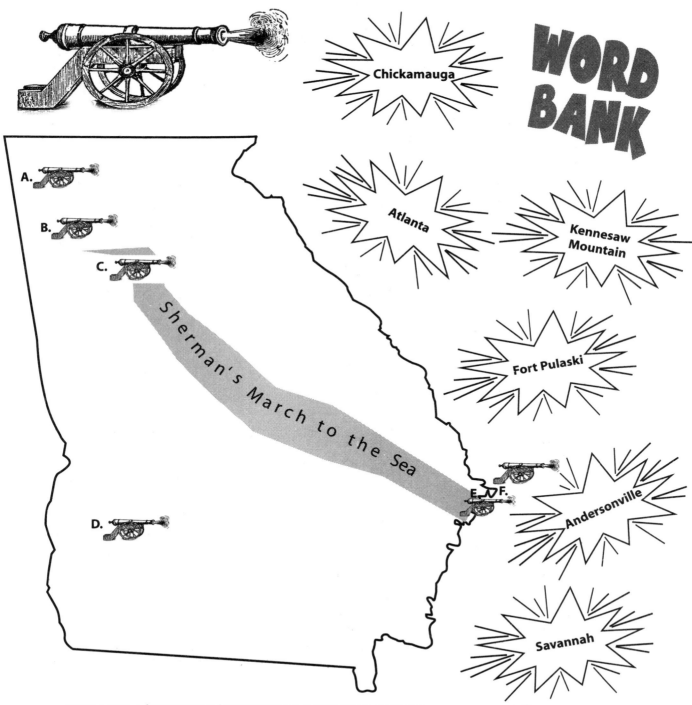

Chickamauga

WORD BANK

Atlanta

Kennesaw Mountain

Fort Pulaski

Sherman's March to the Sea

Andersonville

Savannah

A. B. C. D. E. F.

ANSWERS: A-Chickamauga; B- Kennesaw Mountain; C-Atlanta; D-Andersonville; E-Savannah; F-Fort Pulaski

Meet Joe Black!

Joe Black is a quarrier in the north Georgia mountains. He is strong and works hard. He works in a marble quarry and uses many tools in his job. One is a pick, another is a shovel.

Did you know that Georgia is the world's largest producer of marble? Many of the nation's most famous landmarks were constructed using Georgia marble–including the U.S. Capitol and the Lincoln Monument in Washington, D.C.

Joe is on his way home after working all day, but, whoops, he forgot his tools. Help Joe get back to the quarry to find his missing pick and shovel, and then go home.

Go mining for the other Georgia minerals buried in the marble quarry by accident. Circle them when you strike it rich!

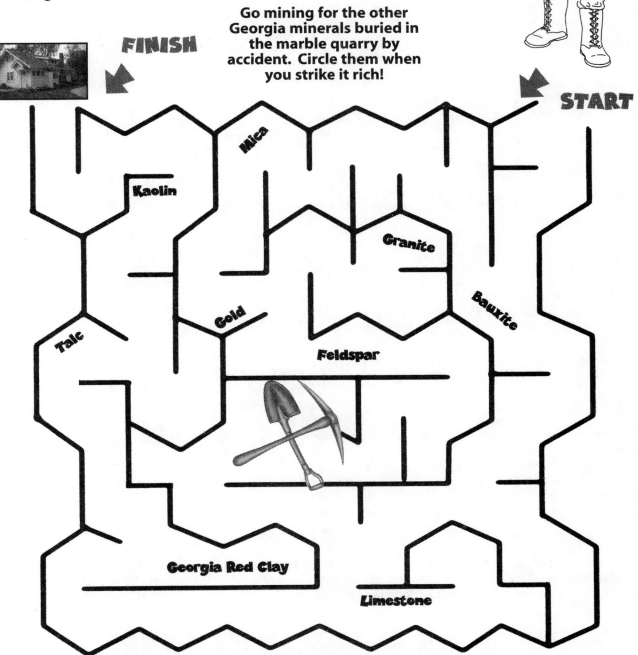

FINISH

START

Mica

Kaolin

Granite

Gold

Bauxite

Talc

Feldspar

Georgia Red Clay

Limestone

Places to go! Things to do!

Georgia has so many cool places to go and so many cool things to do! They're located in the big, busy capital city of Atlanta, in the Blue Ridge Mountains to the north, and at the Atlantic Ocean in the south and east.

Use the Word Bank to help you complete the sentences below and learn about some of the exciting Georgia sites you can visit!

1. You can see dinosaurs and more at _ _ _ _ _ _ _ _ _ Museum of Natural History in Atlanta. While you're there, visit the _ _ _ _ _ _ _ _ _ Science Center and Planetarium to get a closeup look at the stars!

2. *SCREAM* while you're riding the Scream Machine Roller Coaster at _ _ _ _ _ _ _ _ _ _ _ _ _ _ _ _ _ _ in Austell.

3. _ _ _ _ _ _ _ _ in Atlanta is one of the nation's top 10 science centers with interactive exhibits! You can touch and play with everything!

4. At the Atlanta _ you'll not only see a great puppet show—you'll learn lots and lots about the history of puppets and how they work!

5. To be transported back in time to the Civil War, make plans to see the _ _ _ _ _ _ _ _ _ in Grant Park where you'll be surrounded by a circular 400 foot (120 meter) painting of the Battle of Atlanta complete with lifelike figures of Confederate soldiers battling General Sherman and the Union Army. It's a 3-D panorama!

6. Put the State _ _ _ _ _ _ _ _ _ _ _ _ _ _ _ of Georgia in Athens on your list to take a nature walk through beautiful gardens filled with lions and tigers and bears, oh my! Just kidding, but they are filled with trees and flowers and lots and lots of Georgia wildlife!

7. Learn about the 39th President of the United States at the _ _ _ _ _ _ Presidential Library, part of the _ _ _ _ _ _ Center in Atlanta.

8. Pack your swimsuit and sunscreen and head for the beach! Visit Georgia's _ _ _ _ _ _ _ _ _ _ _ _: Ossabaw, Wassaw, St. Catherines, St. Simons, Jekyll, Sea, Sapelo, and Cumberland.

9. Many, many more marvelous _ _ _ _ _ _ _ _ abound in Georgia: High Museum of Art in Atlanta, Harriet Tubman African-American Museum in Columbus, Martin Luther King, Jr. Center in Atlanta, Georgia Mountains History Museum in Gainesville, Telfair Academy of Arts and Sciences in Savannah, Uncle Remus Museum and Park in Eatonton, the Confederate Naval Museum in Columbus, and the National Country Music Museum in Buena Vista, just to name a few!

10. Watch a fast-paced Cable News Network at work while you tour _ _ _ in downtown Atlanta.

WORD BANK

- **Carter (use twice)**
- **Botanical Garden**
- **Scitrek**
- **Fernbank (use twice, too)**
- **Golden Isles**
- **Cyclorama**
- **Six Flags over Georgia**
- **Center for Puppetry Arts**
- **CNN (Cable News Network)**

ANSWER: 1-Fernbank; 2-Six Flags Over Georgia; 3-Scitrek; 4-Center for Puppetry Arts; 5-Cyclorama; 6-State Botanical Garden of Georgia; 7-Carter; 8-Golden Isles; 9-Museums; 10-CNN

Good Golly! Georgia Geography Word Search

Georgia has lots and lots of cities and towns spread all around.

See if you can find these Georgia cities in the Word Search below!

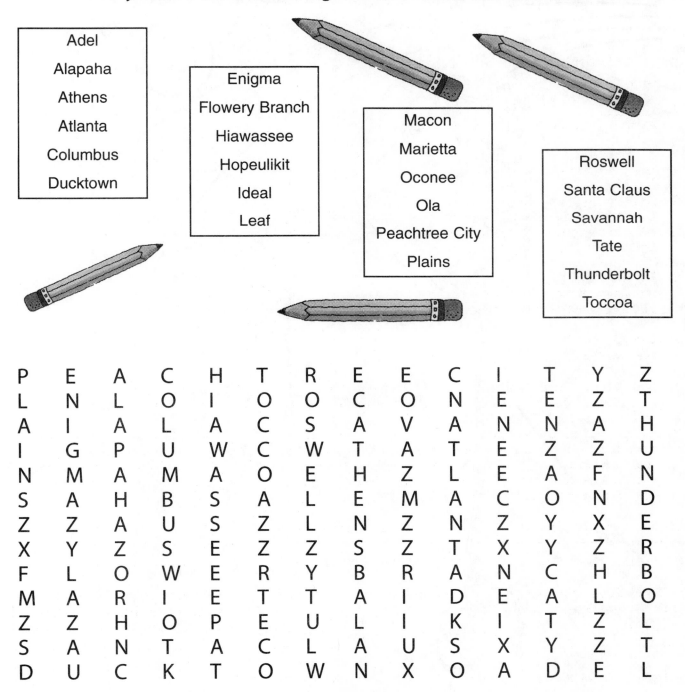

Adel
Alapaha
Athens
Atlanta
Columbus
Ducktown

Enigma
Flowery Branch
Hiawassee
Hopeulikit
Ideal
Leaf

Macon
Marietta
Oconee
Ola
Peachtree City
Plains

Roswell
Santa Claus
Savannah
Tate
Thunderbolt
Toccoa

```
P  E  A  C  H  T  R  E  E  C  I  T  Y  Z
L  N  L  O  I  O  O  C  O  N  E  E  Z  T
A  I  A  L  A  C  S  A  V  A  N  N  A  H
I  G  P  U  W  C  W  T  A  T  E  Z  Z  U
N  M  A  M  A  O  E  H  Z  L  E  A  F  N
S  A  H  B  S  A  L  E  M  A  C  O  N  D
Z  Z  A  U  S  Z  L  N  Z  N  Z  Y  X  E
X  Y  Z  S  E  Z  Z  S  Z  T  X  Y  Z  R
F  L  O  W  E  R  Y  B  R  A  N  C  H  B
M  A  R  I  E  T  T  A  I  D  E  A  L  O
Z  Z  H  O  P  E  U  L  I  K  I  T  Z  L
S  A  N  T  A  C  L  A  U  S  X  Y  Z  T
D  U  C  K  T  O  W  N  X  O  A  D  E  L
```

Olympic Spotlight on Atlanta

In 1996, Atlanta hosted the Summer Olympics. It was a great time for the city, the athletes, and the visitors! You can still visit Centennial Olympic Park in downtown Atlanta and enjoy its dancing waters, lights, and music!

Color the track star and the Olympic Rings!

GEORGIA Rules!

Use the code to complete the sentences.

A	B	C	D	E	F	G	H	I	J	K	L	M	N	O	P	Q	R	S	T
1	2	3	4	5	6	7	8	9	10	11	12	13	14	15	16	17	18	19	20

U	V	W	X	Y	Z
21	22	23	24	25	26

1. State rules are called ___ ___ ___ ___.
   12   1   23   19

2. Laws are made in our state ___ ___ ___ ___ ___ ___ ___.
   3   1   16   9   20   15   12

3. The leader of our state is the ___ ___ ___ ___ ___ ___ ___ ___.
   7   15   22   5   18   14   15   18

4. We live in the state of ___ ___ ___ ___ ___ ___ ___.
   7   5   15   18   7   9   1

5. The capital of our state is ___ ___ ___ ___ ___ ___ ___.
   1   20   12   1   14   20   1

GEORGIA!!!

ANSWERS: 1-Laws; 2-Capitol; 3-Governor; 4-Georgia; 5-Atlanta

Crazy Quilt!

Quilts made by Georgians have become valuable heirlooms. Heirlooms are family possessions handed down from generation to generation. Often a woman would tell a story about her family with the pattern of her quilt.

African-American women included "secret" instructions in the design of their quilts to help slaves escape to freedom on the Underground Railroad!

We've started this quilt just for you...now, you can finish "sewing" the quilt by adding pictures that tell a story about your family. You can even use the lines below to tell a story, too!

_____

_____

_____

_____

Nacoochee Valley!

The Nacoochee Valley is in the northeastern corner of Georgia nestled in the shelter of the Blue Ridge Mountains. This is a region of hardwood and pine forests–birch, hickory, chestnut, oak, walnut, poplar, hemlock, and white pine. Many different species of animals and insects make their homes in the beautiful Nacoochee Valley.

How many of each plant or animal can you find in this school scene?
Write your answers below.

How many?

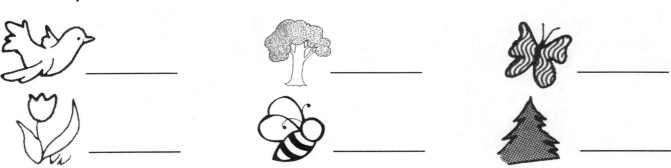

A Georgia Basketful

Match the name of each crop or product from Georgia with the basket full of that item.

Corn   Apples   Tomatoes   Eggs

Crabs and Fish   Corn, Potatoes, Onions, and Peppers

U.S. Time Zones

Would you believe that the United States is divided into four time zones? It is! Because of the rotation of the earth, the sun travels from east to west. Whenever the sun is directly overhead, we call that time noon. But, when it is noon in Atlanta, the sun has a long way to go before it is directly over San Francisco, California. When it is 12:00 pm (noon) in Savannah, it is 11:00 am in Chicago, Illinois. **There is a one-hour time difference between each zone!**

Look at the time zones on the map below, then answer the following questions:

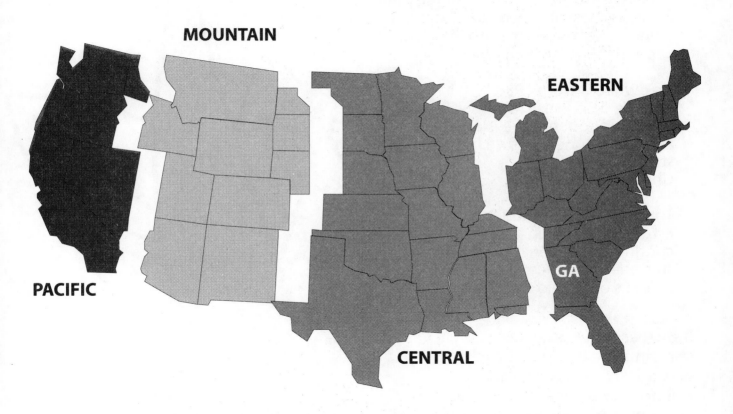

1. When it is 10:00 am in Macon, Georgia what time is it in California? _____ am

2. When it is 3:30 pm in Dahlonega, Georgia what time is it in Ohio? _____ pm

3. What time zone is Georgia located in? _____

4. What time zone is Colorado in? _____

5. If it is 10:00 pm in Valdosta, Georgia what time is it in Alabama? _____ pm

ANSWERS: 1-7:00 am; 2- 3:30 pm; 3. Eastern; 4. Mountain; 5. 9:00 pm

Tobacco and how it ended up on a Golden Isle!

Tobacco is a crop that was grown in early Georgia–and is still grown today.

Tobacco also played a role in one of the islands off the Georgia coast. Tobacco millionaire R.J. Reynolds owned one of Georgia's Golden Isles named Sapelo.

He owned it from 1934 until he died in 1964. Reynolds donated the island and the marine institute he started to the University of Georgia.

The Sapelo Island National Estuarine Research Reserve continues the work that Reynolds started—the study of plants and animals of Sapelo's wetlands.

Below are four pictures showing the economic cycle of a tobacco crop. Number the boxes below in the correct order.

TO MARKET

"Stone" Mountain Men!

Stone Mountain (east of Atlanta) is one of the world's largest exposed granite rocks. It rises 650 feet (195 meters) and covers 2 square miles (5.2 square kilometers). A carving of three historical Civil War figures—Jefferson Davis (president of the Confederacy), General Robert E. Lee, and General "Stonewall" Jackson—graces the northern face. The carving, started in 1923, took almost 50 years to complete.

You can take a tram up–up–up to the very top of the mountain, or you can put your hiking shoes on and walk all the way!

Draw a line from the names to the figures on the mountain. Check your answers below!

"STONEWALL" JACKSON

ROBERT E. LEE

JEFFERSON DAVIS

Visit between Memorial Day and Labor Day and see an exciting laser and sound show with really great fireworks!

Carvers working on the sculpture took shelter from rain storms inside the horses' mouths— pretty big carving, huh!

ANSWERS: Left to right–President Jefferson Davis; General Robert E. Lee; President "Stonewall" Jackson

Georgia's Venomous Snakes!

Four species of venomous (poisonous) snakes live in Georgia.

Using the alphabet code, see if you can find out their names.
Use the code to complete the sentences.

A	B	C	D	E	F	G	H	I	J	K	L	M	N	O	P	Q	R	S	T
1	2	3	4	5	6	7	8	9	10	11	12	13	14	15	16	17	18	19	20

U	V	W	X	Y	Z
21	22	23	24	25	26

1. __ __ __ __ __   __ __ __ __ __
    3 15 18 1 12   19 14 1 11 5

2. __ __ __ __ __   __ __ __ __ __ __ __ __
    23 1 20 5 18   13 15 3 3 1 19 9 14

3. __ __ __ __ __ __ __ __ __ __
    3 15 16 16 5 18 8 5 1 4

4. __ __ __ __ __ __ __ __ __ __ __
    4 9 1 13 15 14 4 2 1 3 11

    __ __ __ __ __ __ __ __ __ __ __
    18 1 20 20 12 5 19 14 1 11 5

Claxton has its very own Rattlesnake Roundup that's held every March. You can slither on up and see some crafts, a parade, and even some cloggers! OOH watch out for those tap shoes!

ANSWERS: 1- Coral Snake; 2-Water Moccasin; 3-Copperhead; 4-Diamondback Rattlesnake

Georgie's 2 Many Peaches Day!

Count all the "2s" in the story and
write your total in the box below:

Georgie was a young Fort Valley colonist. He was interested in the peach crop they were growing. Perhaps, he was 2 interested!

"If you want 2 help," said his father, "you can put on these 2 gloves and pull the peaches from these 2 rows of peach trees."

Georgie began 2 work. He worked on 2 trees. He finished 2 trees. Then he tackled another 2 trees, then another 2. Then Georgie decided that the sun was 2 hot and he was 2 tired and this was not 2 much fun after all!

His friends began 2 tease him. "You are working 2 hard," they said. "We are having 2 much fun. Don't you want 2 join us?"

"My father has 2 much work 2 do," Georgie said. "But I have worked 2 hours and so I will take a 2 minute break with you."

I counted this many 2s:

Big & Busy Hartsfield!

The big and busy Atlanta Hartsfield International Airport has the world's largest terminal and serves more than 73,000,000 passengers a year! *Whew!* That's a lot of planes taking off and landing!

Many different airlines fly in and out of Atlanta every day–Delta, US Airways, American, United, America West, British Airways, Northwest, Trans World–to name a few.

See all the planes and things heading for Hartsfield?
Circle all of the ones you think would be landing there today!

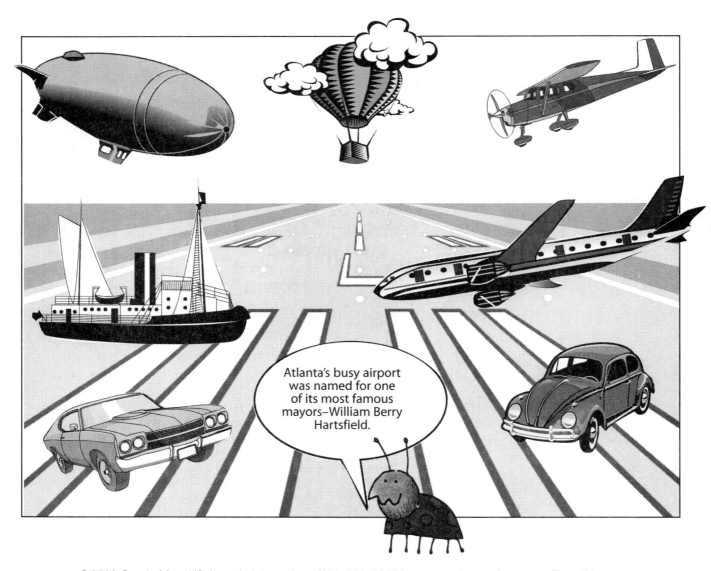

You Can't Fool Foal!

"My name is Foal. I help tend the wild horses that live on Georgia's Cumberland Island. The horses I help take care of have funny names like Paint Spot and Willy. I've heard they're descendants of horses left by Spanish explorers in the 1600s. All I know is that I love the horses, and they love me! Maybe that's because I give them treats like apples and sugar!"

"I also like to go to Sapelo Island and visit the candy-cane striped lighthouse."

Color the Sapelo Island Lighthouse red where indicated.

Add spots to Foal's favorite horse, Paint Spot!

red

red

red

Georgia's First Christmas!

In colonial days, a cornucopia, or "horn of plenty," decorated the Christmas table. How does your family decorate your holiday table?

Color the cornucopia as follows:

Georgia Indians!

Creek, Cherokee, and Yamasee Indians were the first people living in Georgia. They lived in the New World before the explorers and colonists came.

Circle the things that Indians might have used in their everyday life.

Some Patriotic Holidays

FLAG DAY

Flag Day is celebrated on June 14 to honor our flag. Our country's flag is an important symbol. It makes us proud of our country. It makes us proud to be Americans.

Count the number of stars and stripes on the flag.

_____ Stars   _____ Stripes

MEMORIAL DAY

Memorial Day is also known as Decoration Day. We remember the people who died in wars and fought so that we could be free.

Circle the things you might put on a grave on Memorial Day.

VETERANS DAY

On Veterans Day we recognize Americans who served in the armed forces.

Circle ways we celebrate Veterans Day.

Getting There From Here!

Methods of transportation have changed in Georgia from the days of early explorers and the time when colonists arrived and found Native Americans already living in Georgia.

Match each person to the way they would travel.

Native American

race car driver

child

colonist

astronaut

early explorer

pilot

Georgia Word Wheel

From the Word Wheel of Georgia names, answer the following questions.

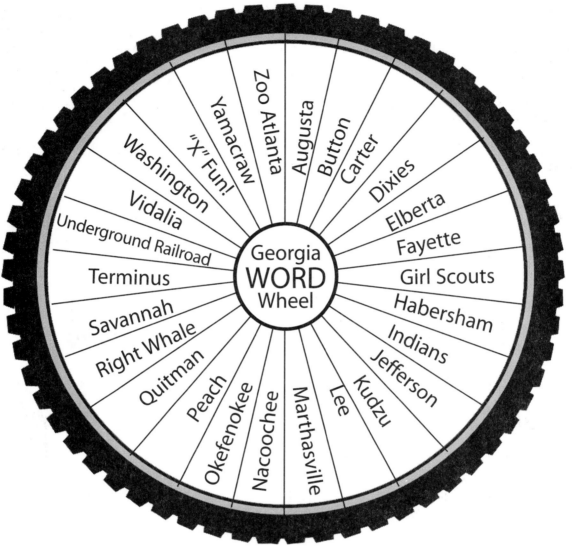

1. The 39th president of the United States was Jimmy _____.
2. General Robert E. _____ was a Confederate general in the Civil War.
3. The first people to live in Georgia were _____.
4. One of Georgia's nicknames is the _____ State.
5. James Oglethorpe and British settlers landed at _____ Bluff.
6. The _____ Swamp sprawls across the Georgia–Florida border.
7. _____ was a Cherokee Princess.
8. _____ Gwinnett signed the Declaration of Independence.
9. Atlanta was originally named _____ and _____.
10. _____ is the name of a famous onion and the town that developed it.

Alligators Abound
in the Okefenokee

Alligators live in freshwater wetlands. One of their favorite "homes" is the Okefenokee Swamp that covers 438,000 acres (175,200 hectares) in southeastern Georgia and northeastern Florida. Okefenokee is a Seminole Indian word meaning *"trembling earth."* The Okefenokee is the second largest freshwater swamp in the U.S. with islands, lakes, and prairies separated by moss-covered forests. There are layers of peat deposits covered by grasses, shrubs, and trees—which is why the earth does indeed *tremble* when you walk on it!

When you visit the Okefenokee Swamp, you'll have an opportunity to see lots and lots of alligators—it's the place 15,000 of them call home, sweet home!

You can make at least 15 words from the letters in ALLIGATOR.
See if you can find all 15–or more!

_____   _____   _____

_____   _____   _____

_____   _____   _____

_____   _____   _____

_____   _____   _____

You found how many words? WOW that's awesome!

A President from Plains

James Earl Carter
The Thirty-Ninth U.S. President

Jimmy Carter was a career naval officer who resigned from the Navy to manage his family's peanut business in Plains, Georgia. He was governor of Georgia and later became the 39th President of the United States.

As president, Jimmy Carter worked hard with other nations for human rights. He is still very active in the fight for human life!

In 1943, Georgia became the first state to allow 18-year olds the right to vote!

The legal age to vote in Georgia is 18. Let's see how long it'll be be before you'll be able to cast your vote:

18	
- _____	Write your age here.
	Subtract to find out how many years it will be before you can cast your vote!

A Zoo for You and Pandas, too!

Zoo Atlanta, near downtown Atlanta, has two very special guests—Lun Lun and Yang Yang! They are Giant Pandas on loan to the zoo from China. They'll be here until 2010, so come and visit!

While we're visiting the zoo, let's learn a thing *or two* about Giant Pandas!

Giant Pandas come from the mountains of Asia. They can grow to 6 feet (1.8 meters) and weigh 220 pounds (100 kg). Their main food is bamboo. Giant Pandas don't hibernate since their food supply is available all year. They'll eat up to 90 pounds (40 kg) of juicy bamboo shoots every day, and they'll take about 16 hours a day filling their tummies. Babies are usually born in August or September weighing only 2.5 to 5 ounces (75-150 g). But, they grow fast–up to 75 pounds (35 kg) by the time they're a year old!

Giant Pandas are very special animals. They are endangered! We must be very careful to protect them, so that they do not become extinct and lost to us forever!

Now–here's the really fun part! See if you can answer the following questions about Zoo Atlanta's special guests:

1. What are the names of the two Giant Pandas on loan to Zoo Atlanta?
   _____ and _____
2. How tall can they grow?_____
3. Where do Giant Pandas come from?_____
4. What food do they like best?_____
5. When are babies usually born?_____
6. Why are Giant Pandas so special?_____

ANSWERS: 1-Lun Lun and Yang Yang; 2-6 feet (1.8 meters); 3-Mountains of Asia; 4-Bamboo; 5-August or September; 6-Because they're an endangered species!

What Shall I Be When I Grow Up?

Here are just a few of the jobs that kept early Georgians busy.

Lawyer	Tenant Farmer	Woodcarver
Judge	Housekeeper	Silversmith
Politician	Dairyman	Wheelwright
Teacher	Servant	Cabinetmaker
Mayor	Plantation Owner	Cooper (barrelmaker)
Carpenter	Weaver	Barber
Gardener	Mantuamaker (dressmaker)	Printer
Cook	Musician	Bookbinder
Laundress	Jeweler	Innkeeper
Stablehand	Tailor	Minister
Baker	Pharmacist	Gaoler (jailer)
Fisherman	Doctor	Governor
Crabber	Milliner (hatmaker)	Soldier
Hunter	Blacksmith	Sailor
Beekeeper	Gunsmith	Prospector

You are a young colonist trying to decide what you want to be when you grow up.

Choose a career and next to it write a description of what you think you would do each day as a:

Write your career choice here!

_____

_____
_____
_____

Write your career choice here!

_____

_____
_____
_____

Write your career choice here!

_____

_____
_____
_____

Write your career choice here!

_____

_____
_____
_____

Producers and Consumers

Producers (sellers) make goods or provide services. Ralph, a 4th grade student in Atlanta, is a consumer because he wants to buy a new wheel for his bicycle.

Help Ralph locate the bicycle-wheel seller so he can fix his bike!

MALL MANIA!

HISTORIC UNDERGROUND ATLANTA–PART OF ATLANTA THAT WASN'T TORCHED BY GENERAL SHERMAN AND HIS TROOPS DURING THE CIVIL WAR–IS NOW A POPULAR UNDERGROUND SHOPPING MALL!

ATTENTION SHOPPERS: Did you know that, after Chicago, Atlanta has more shopping center space per person than any other U.S. city?

BOY! You should see the parking lots during holiday shopping!

Dr. Martin Luther King, Jr.

Dr. Martin Luther King, Jr. was born in Atlanta in 1929. He was a Baptist preacher and very eloquent speaker. He and his father preached at Ebenezer Baptist Church on Auburn Avenue in Atlanta.

Dr. King worked very hard for equal rights for all Americans. His dream was to make African-Americans "free at last."

His philosophy was nonviolent and peaceful resistance. His message for civil rights was heard around the world, and in 1964, Dr. King was awarded the Nobel Peace Prize.

In April 1968, Dr. King was assassinated as he stood on the balcony of the Lorraine Motel in Memphis, Tennessee. Dr. King's tomb lies at the Martin Luther King, Jr. Center in Atlanta, just a block from his home on Auburn Avenue.

Congress established the third Monday in January as a federal holiday in honor of Dr. King's birthday.

Color the picture of Dr. Martin Luther King, Jr.

A-MAZE-ING Commute!

A lot of Georgians work for the federal and state government in Atlanta.
Help the MARTA train find the quickest way to the capitol. ZOOM!!!

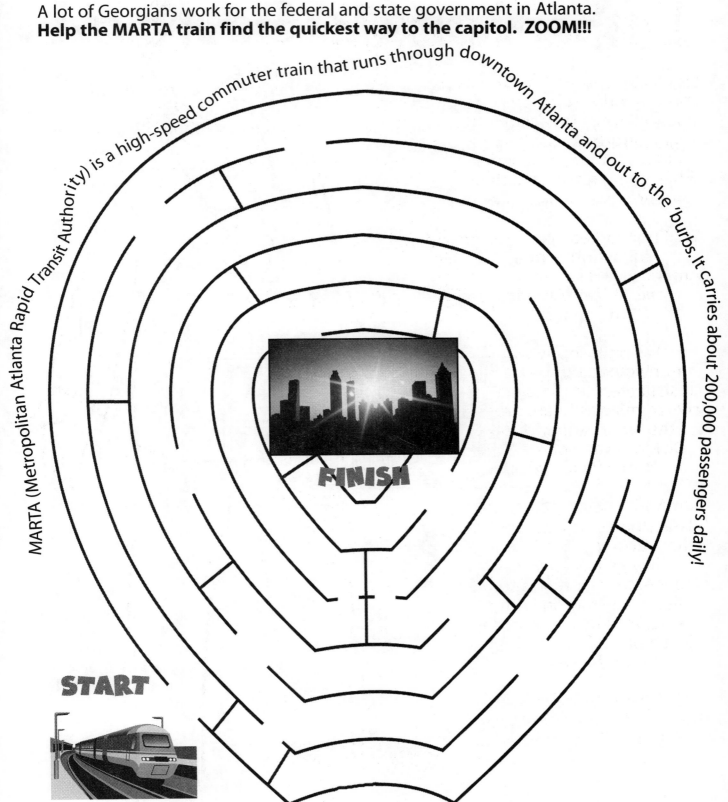

MARTA (Metropolitan Atlanta Rapid Transit Authority) is a high-speed commuter train that runs through downtown Atlanta and out to the 'burbs. It carries about 200,000 passengers daily!

START

FINISH

African Slaves Come to Georgia

When Georgia was founded in 1733 by Englishman James E. Oglethorpe, slave labor was prohibited. The plantation owners demanded that they be allowed to have slaves to plant, grow, and harvest the crops. In 1750, the Georgia trustees (men who ran the state) agreed and slave trade was allowed. Men, women, and children were brought by ship from Africa to work.

Locate Africa on the map . . . . Write an **"S"** for Slaves
Locate the United States on the map . . . . Write an **"L"** for Labor
Locate the Atlantic Ocean . . . . Write an **"A"*** on the Atlantic Ocean
Locate Georgia on the map . . . . Write a **"V"** for Georgia
Draw a line from Africa to Georgia .   .   Write an **"E"** for expansion

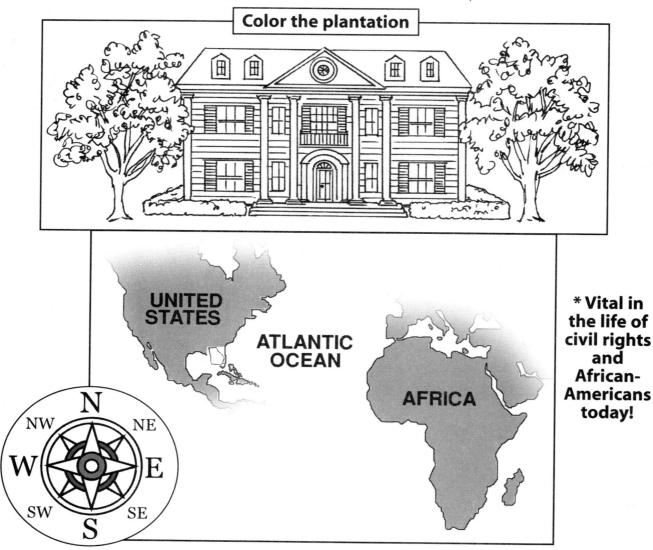

Color the plantation

UNITED STATES

ATLANTIC OCEAN

AFRICA

***** Vital in the life of civil rights and African-Americans today!**

Rainbow, Pretty Rainbow

Rainbows often appear over the Georgia countryside after a storm. Rainbows are formed when sunlight bends through raindrops. Big raindrops produce the brightest, most beautiful rainbows. You can see rainbows early or late on a rainy day when the sun is behind you.

Color the rainbow in the order of colors listed below, starting at the top of the rainbow.

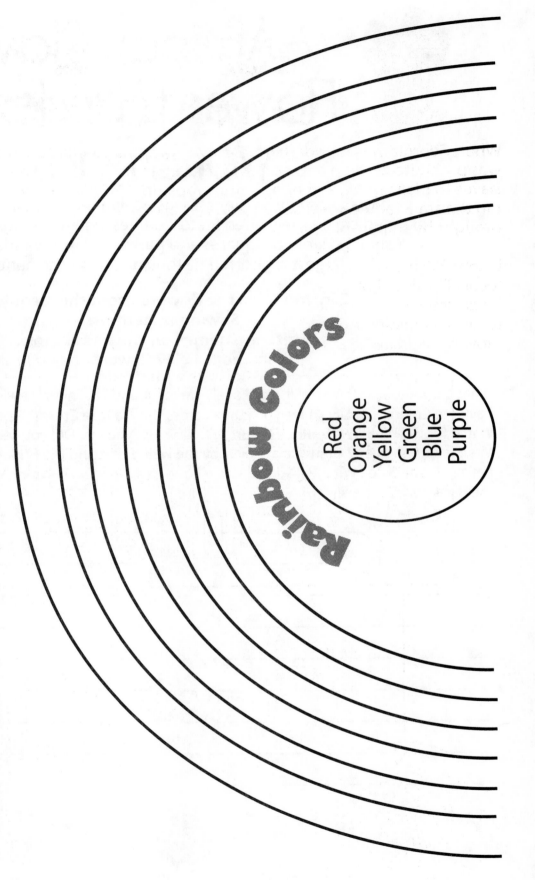

Rainbow Colors

Red
Orange
Yellow
Green
Blue
Purple

Flower Garden Word Find

Georgia's first city, Savannah, was a "planned city." It was the first planned city in the United States! James Oglethorpe drew the plans using a system of squares and parks. Today, Savannah has the largest registered historic district in the nation.

**Can you "pick the flowers" from this beautiful
Savannah garden?
Write the names on the lines below.**
(Hint: There are 17 flowers named.)

What a good boy is Sweet William! Lovely Larkspur and Lavender. Lewis and Clark brought back the Columbian Lily. Have you come across the Maltese Cross? Tiptoe through the Trillium. Watch for the White Wake-Robin. Hurrah for the Hollyhocks. Did you see Johnny-Jump-Up? Mrs. Sinkins and Lady Granville are over by the wall discussing the Bridal Veil. Is it Fair Folly to believe in the Essex Witch? Did you know Love-Lies-Bleeding? Put on your Joseph's Coat with the Bachelor's Buttons!

_____   _____

_____   _____

_____   _____

_____   _____

_____   _____

_____   _____

_____   _____

_____

ANSWERS: Sweet William; Lovely Larkspur; Lavender; Columbian Lily; Maltese Cross; Trillium; White Wake-Robin; Hollyhocks; Johnny-Jump-Up; Mrs. Sinkins; Lady Granville; Bridal Veil; Fair Folly; Essex Witch; Love-Lies-Bleeding; Joseph's Coat; Bachelor's Buttons

Bad Dude Blackbeard

Edward Teach, better known as Blackbeard was called the "fiercest pirate of them all!" The infamous pirate often visited Georgia's shores. Blackbeard Island is one of Georgia's coastal islands on the Atlantic Ocean. It is named after the pirate, who some say, buried treasure here. In 1940, Blackbeard Island was designated a national wildlife refuge to protect native wildlife and migratory birds.

Do you think his treasure might be buried somewhere on the island?

Color the Treasure Chest.
Woodgrain=brown
Trim=yellow
Round Jewels=blue and green

Add all the booty (treasure) inside you want!

Geographic Tools

Beside each item you need to accomplish, put the initials of the tool that can best help you!

(CR) Compass Rose   (LL) Longitude and Latitude
(M) Map   (G) Grid
(K) Map key/legend

1. _____ I need to find the geographic location of Germany.

2. _____ I need to learn where an airport is located near Columbus.

3. _____ I need to find which way is north.

4. _____ I need to chart a route from Georgia to California.

5. _____ I need to find a small town on a map.

Match the items on the left with the items on the right.

1. Grid system
2. Compass rose
3. Longitude and latitude
4. Two of Georgia's borders
5. Symbols on a map

A. Map key or legend
B. Alabama and the Atlantic Ocean
C. A system of letters and numbers
D. Imaginary lines around the earth
E. Shows N, S, E, and W

ANSWERS: 1- LL; 2-K; 3-CR; 4-M; 5-G;
1-C; 2-E; 3-D; 4-B; 5-A

$ Macon's Making Money $

In early America, there were no banks. However, people still needed to get goods from each other. They would "barter" or swap goods or services. "I'll give you a chicken and you bake some bread for me." Later, banks came into existence, and people began to use money, but they still bartered when they had no money to spend.

Draw two pairs of shoes in the window for the shoemaker.
Draw two loaves of bread in the window of the bakery.
Draw a hammer in the blacksmith's window.
Draw a dress in the window for the dressmaker.
Draw a saddle in the saddlemaker's window.
Draw a sack of flour and a teapot in the storekeeper's window.

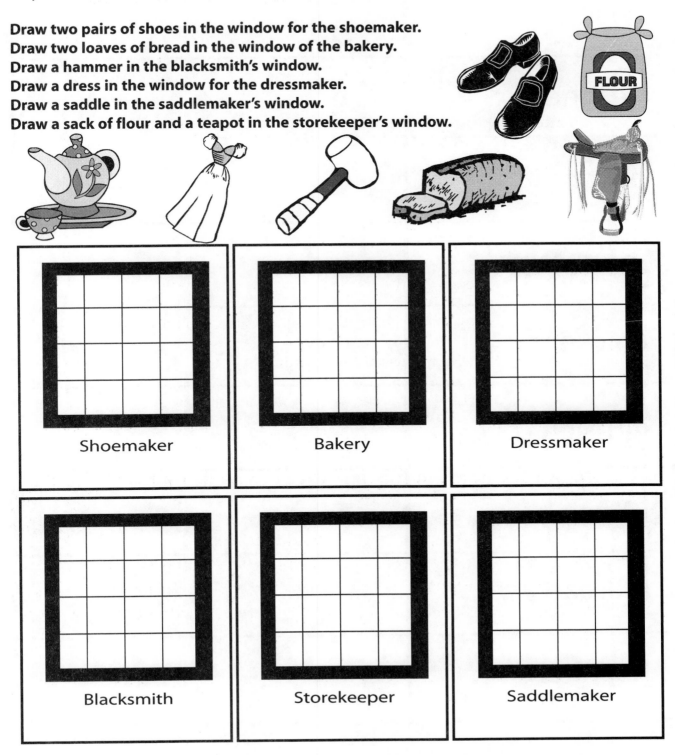

Shoemaker

Bakery

Dressmaker

Blacksmith

Storekeeper

Saddlemaker

Map Symbols

Make up symbols for these names and draw them in the space provided on right.

peanuts	
peaches	
pecans	
mountains	
chickens	
airport	
fort	
railroad	
hospital	

Battledore Goes Into Battle!

"Hi, my name is Battledore. This is my dog, Tin Whistle. We are soldiers in the Civil War. We are fighting for the Confederate Army. I am from Georgia. So is Tin Whistle. I don't know what war is all about yet. I thought I wanted to fight, but now I'm not so sure. I'm homesick. Tonight I will sleep in a tent beside a creek called Chickamauga. Tomorrow, I will fight in my first battle. I am excited and afraid. Wish me luck!"

Draw Battledore's tent below. Put a stack of cannonballs beside it. Also draw a campfire with a pot of beans simmering on it. Help him get ready for the big battle at Chickamauga Creek.

The Battle of Chickamauga Creek, in northwestern Georgia, was the bloodiest two days of the Civil War and ended in a Confederate victory! General Braxton Bragg led the Confederates and General William Rosecrans led the Union soldiers in this famous battle!

Mixed-Up States!

Color, cut out, and paste each of Georgia's six neighbors onto the map of the Southeast.

Be sure and match the state shapes!

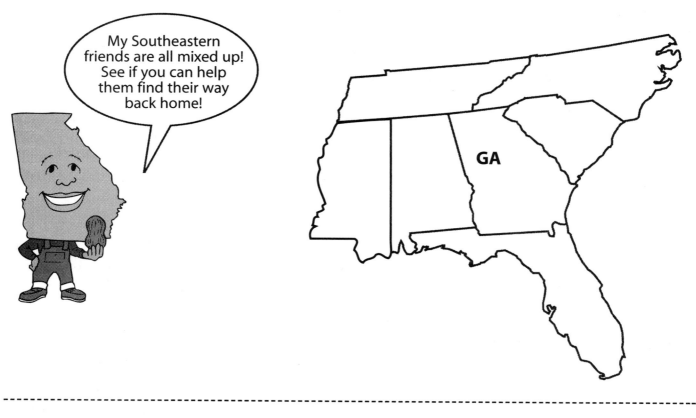

My Southeastern friends are all mixed up! See if you can help them find their way back home!

GA

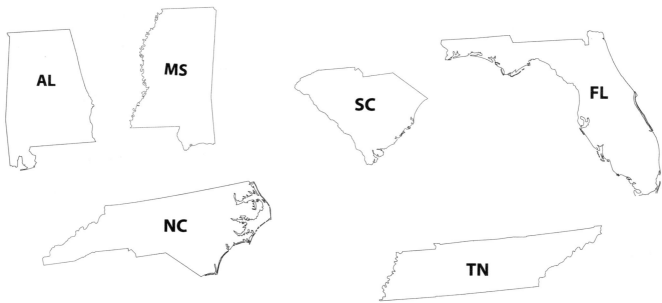

AL

MS

SC

FL

NC

TN

Politics As Usual

Our elected government officials decide how much money is going to be spent on schools, roads, public parks, and libraries. It's very important for the citizens of the state to understand what's going on in their government and how it will affect them. Below are some political words that are often used when talking about government.

MATCH THESE POLITICAL WORDS WITH THEIR DEFINITION

A

1._____ Constitution

2._____ Governor

3._____ Chief Justice

4._____ General Assembly

5._____ District

6._____ Amendment

7._____ Term

8._____ Election

9._____ Veto

10._____ Bill

B

A. Number of years that an elected official is elected to serve

B. Lead Judge on the State Supreme Court

C. The chief executive; cannot serve more than two consecutive terms

D. An addition to the Constitution

E. The selection, by vote, of a candidate for office

F. Georgia's law-making body, made up of the House of Representatives and the Senate

G. Written in 1777, this document established Georgia's state laws

H. The ability to forbid a bill or law from being passed

I. Draft of a law presented for review

J. A division of a state for the purpose of electing a representative from that division

Answers: 1-G; 2-C; 3-B; 4-F; 5-J; 6-D; 7-A; 8-E; 9-H; 10-I

People and Their Jobs!

Can you identify these people and their jobs?

Put an A by the person working on a Georgia farm.
Put a B by the people working at a Georgia military installation.
Put a C by the Georgia Olympic athlete.
Put a D by the person working in a granite quarry in northern Georgia.
Put an E by the person working for a high-tech computer company in Atlanta.
Put an F by the person that works on a boat on Georgia's Atlantic coast.

States All Around!
Code-Buster

Decipher the code and write in the names of the states that border Georgia.

A	B	C	D	E	F	G	H	I	J	K	L	M	N	O	P	Q	R

S	T	U	V	W	X	Y	Z

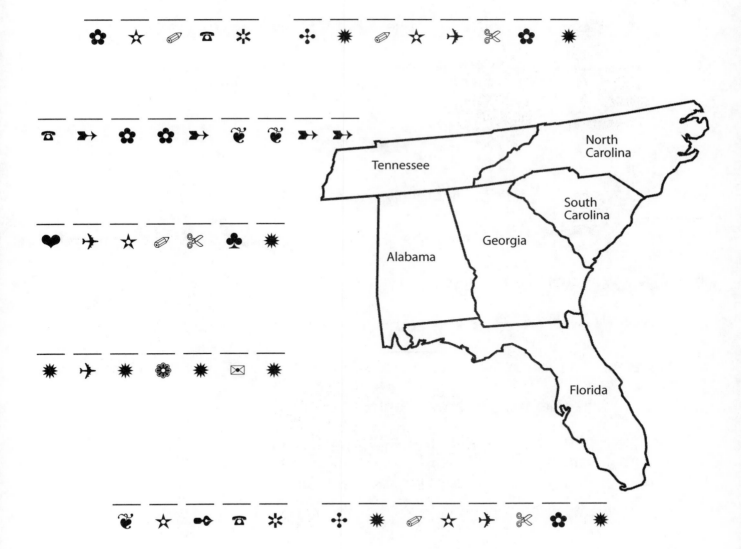

North
Carolina

Tennessee

South
Carolina

Alabama

Georgia

Florida

ANSWERS: North Carolina; Tennessee; Florida; Alabama; South Carolina

©2000 Carole Marsh/Gallopade International/800-536-2GET/www.georgiaexperience.com/Page 87

Ginny of St. Simons Island

 lived in GA .  lived on St. Simons Island in the

Coastal Plain Region near the  . She liked to

 on the  and pick up . Her favorite thing to

do was  . She would put on her and . The

weather was usually , but some days it would  .

Ginny's mother was a at a  on St. Simons and her father

was a . On Saturday, her family had a . Ginny's favorite

food was a . For dessert, she liked to buy an  . Her family drove in

their  through the Marshes of Glynn. They drove north on I-95 to Sapelo

Island to visit the red candy-cane striped . Then, they drove south again on I-95

to visit Cumberland Island. They wanted to see the that roam the island.

loved the wild horses and wished she could have a of her very

own. Ginny and her family had to make plans early to visit Cumberland Island,

because only 300 people per day are allowed to visit.

 liked living in GA at the .

Blast from the Past!

The Shark Tooth is Georgia's state fossil. It's found in the Coastal Plain and comes in a range of colors—black, gray, white, brown, blue, and reddish brown. In fossil form, the Shark Tooth can be traced back 375,000,000 years! **WOW! That's really old!**

Color Georgia's state fossil.

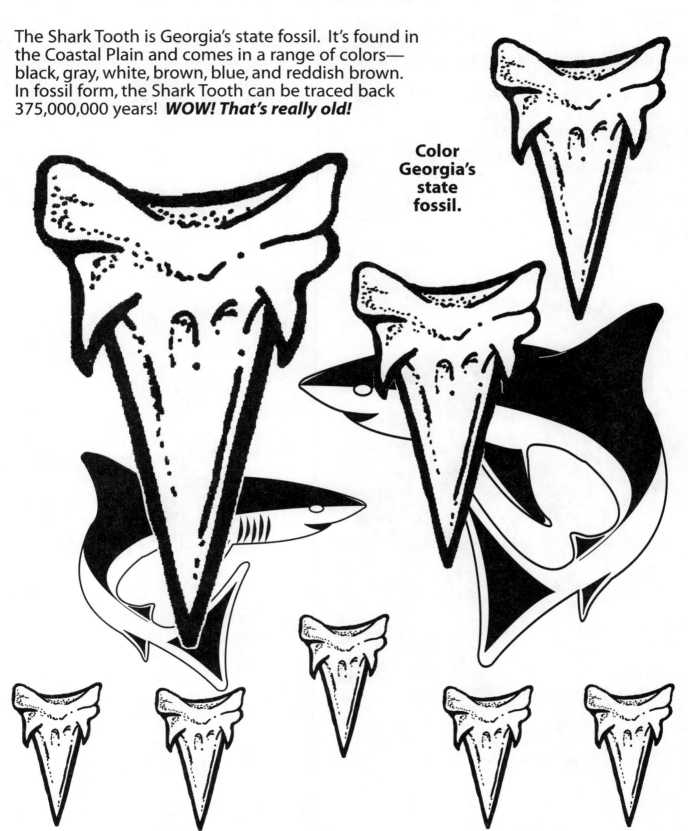

Bees and Trees

Georgia's state insect is the Honeybee *(Apis mellifera)*. Orange and black striped bees contribute to Georgia's economy by producing honey and cross-pollinating over 50 state crops.

Georgia's state tree is the Live Oak *(Quercus virginiana)*. The beautiful Live Oak is found in the Coastal Plain and is usually draped with strands of Spanish moss. It's called a "live" oak because the leaves are green year-round. The average age is said to be 300 years.

1. Why is the Honeybee important to Georgia's economy?

_____

_____.

2. The scientific *(or Latin)* name for Honeybee is _____

_____.

3. Why is Georgia's state tree called the Live Oak?

_____

_____

_____.

4. Where are Live Oaks found in Georgia?

_____

_____.

5. The scientific *(or Latin)* name for the Live Oak is _____

_____.

Colonist, Colonist, What Shall I Wear?

In early Georgia, colonists dressed much as they had back in England. Working men wore knee-length breeches with long stockings, shirts, and vests. Women wore skirts, petticoats, and blouses. They tied a pouch on a string around their waists over their aprons to serve as a "pocket." Women generally wore mob caps of white cloth, often beneath a straw hat. Women wore hats indoors and out. In Savannah, you might have seen men in wigs wearing three-cornered cocked (tricorn) hats. These were sometimes decorated with ostrich plumes or pheasant feathers and colorful ribbon rosettes called cockades. Children dressed much like adults. (I'll bet they would have liked tee shirts!)

Draw a line from each word to its correct place on the characters.

Petticoat

Tricorn Hat

Mob Cap

Blouse

Stockings

Apron

Wig

Breeches

In colonial times, cats did not wear clothes!

Georgia Word Wheel— Give It Another Spin!

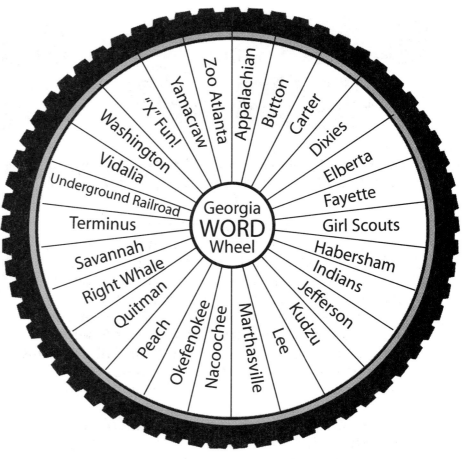

From the Word Wheel of Georgia names, answer the following questions.

1. _____ is Georgia's first city.

2. _____ is the name of Georgia's first famous peach.

3. During the Civil War, Harriet Tubman helped slaves escape on the _____ _____.

4. Juliette Gordon Low founded the _____ _____.

5. _____ Trail is the name of the world's longest continuous mountain trail that starts at Mt. Katahdin in Maine and winds its way down to Georgia's Springer Mountain.

6. _____ is a plant that's a member of the bean family. It was originally brought to Georgia as cattle feed and to help prevent soil erosion.

7. _____ Davis was President of the Confederate States.

8. The _____ _____ is the Marine Mammal of Georgia. They were nearly hunted to extinction in the 1800s and remain rare today!

9. Banks used to issue their own paper notes as currency. The nickname, _____, was given to this money. Later, *Dixie* was a nickname used for the Confederacy (the entire South).

10. Out of the Hills of _____, down the valleys of Hall are the opening lines of Sidney Lanier's famous poem entitled, *Song of the Chattahoochee.*

ANSWERS: 1-Savannah; 2-Elberta; 3-Underground Railroad; 4-Girl Scouts; 5-Appalachian; 6-Kudzu; 7-Jefferson; 8-Right Whale; 9-Dixies; 10-Habersham

Slavery in Georgia:
Nothing to Be Proud Of

While not all farmers owned slaves, some plantation owners could only enlarge their farms with slave labor. African men, women, and children were brought to Georgia and sold as slaves to plantation owners. Slaveowners were sometimes cruel to their slaves. Many slaves tried to escape with the help of people who thought slavery was wrong. Harriet Tubman was a famous African-American who helped slaves escape on the Underground Railroad.

In 1863, U.S. President Abraham Lincoln issued the Emancipation Proclamation which freed the slaves in areas still under Confederate control.

Help the slave escape by using the code to decipher the message.

Key: 1=A, 2=B, 3=C, 5=E, 8=H,
9=I, 13=M, 14=N, 15=O,
16=P, 18=R, 19=S, 20=T

13-5-5-20   9-14   20-8-5   2-1-18-14

20-15   5-19-3-1-16-5.

ANSWER: Meet in the barn to escape.

Local Government

Georgia government, like our national government, is made up of three branches. Each branch has a certain job to do. Each branch also has some power over the other branches. We call this system checks and balances.

See if you can match each official with the correct branch of government.

Made up of the General Assembly which has two houses, the Senate and the House of Representatives. This branch makes and repeals laws.	The Government leaders made up of the Governor, as well as appointed and elected state officials. This branch makes sure that the laws are enforced.	The court system, includes local, district and state courts. This branch interprets the laws.
A. Legislative Branch	**B. Executive Branch**	**C. Judicial Branch**

1. The Governor _____

2. A local district representative _____

3. A member of the General Assembly _____

4. An appointed trustee of a state university _____

5. The Chief Justice of the State Supreme Court _____

6. The speaker of the House of Representatives _____

7. The Lieutenant Governor _____

8. A municipal court judge _____

9. A District Attorney _____

10. A Senator _____

Did you know Georgia has 56 senators?

Yes, and we have 180 state representatives!

ANSWERS: 1-B; 2-A; 3-A; 4-B; 5-C; 6-A; 7-B; 8-C; 9-C; 10-A

Unique Georgia Place Names

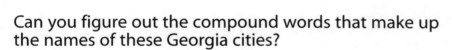

Can you figure out the compound words that make up the names of these Georgia cities?

Stockbridge	Lovejoy	Summertown
_____ _____	_____ _____	_____ _____
Thunderbolt	Doerun	Riverside
_____ _____	_____ _____	_____ _____
Cedartown	Youngcane	Deepstep
_____ _____	_____ _____	_____ _____
Ringgold	Springfield	Stillmore
_____ _____	_____ _____	_____ _____
Blackshear	Newborn	Buckhead
_____ _____	_____ _____	_____ _____
	Fairburn	Flintstone
	_____ _____	_____ _____
	Stonewall	Inman
	_____ _____	_____ _____

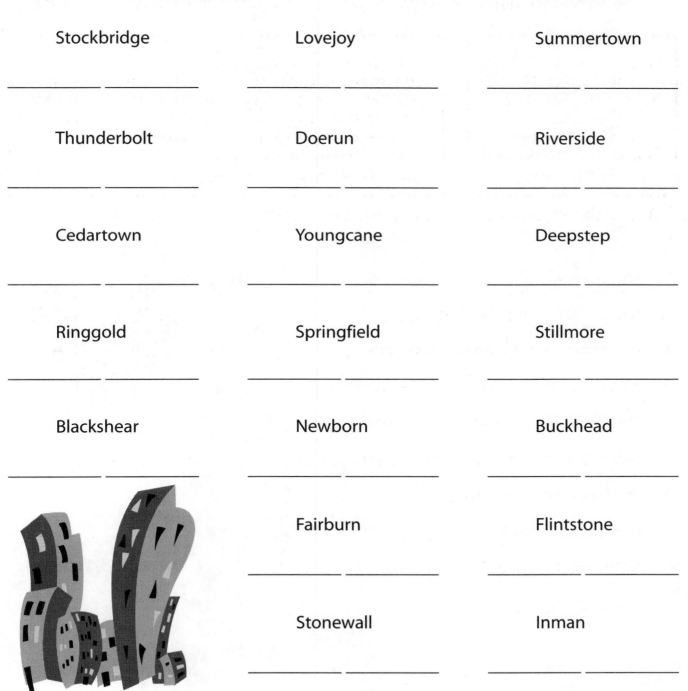

Three Ps and a V!

Georgia leads the nation in the production of peanuts (top cash crop) and pecans. About 1/2 of all peanuts (about 800 billion a year) and 1/3 of all pecans are grown here. Georgia is one of the nation's leading producers of peaches–growing about 40 different kinds today!

Color the picture of Buddy getting ready for a big day on a Georgia farm!

The Vidalia Sweet Onion is named for the town of Vidalia where it was developed in 1931. Vidalias can only be grown properly in a small area of Georgia–a 20 county region that provides the rights soils and mild temperatures that give Vidalias their wonderfully sweet flavor.

I'm #1!

Painted Turtle

Painted turtles live in waterways all across North America, from the east coast of Georgia to the West Coast of North America. They can grow 10 inches long.

"Paint" this turtle using the color key.

COLOR KEY

R = red   B = blue
Y = yellow G = green

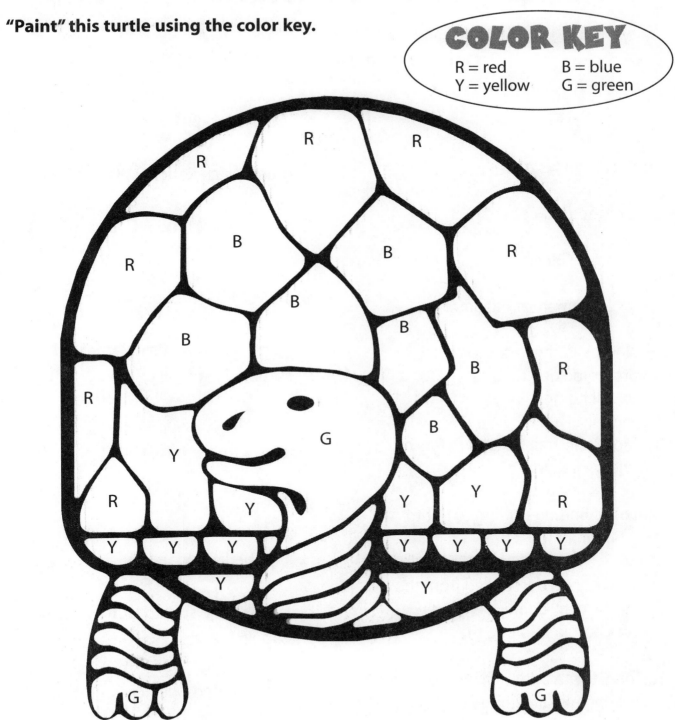

How many spots are on this turtle? _____

ANSWER: 29

Looking For a Home!

Draw a line from the things on the left to their homes on the right!

1. Runaway Chicken

2. Cyclist on his bike

3. Lighthouse Keeper

4. Georgia Ghost

5. 15,000 American Alligators

6. Herons, White Ibis, and Wood Storks looking for a safe place to call home

7. Mountain Trail Hiker with lots of energy and lots of time

8. Lost commuter trying to get to work on time

9. Wild horses descended from those left by early Spanish explorers on Georgia's Golden Isles

10. Tourist with a camera who enjoys visiting historic Civil War sites

11. Prospector looking for gold

A. Duck Pond Bike Path

B. Harris Neck National Wildlife Refuge

C. Gainesville Chicken Coop (Poultry Capital of the World)

D. I-85 or I-75 through Atlanta

E. Kennesaw Mountain Battlefield National Park

F. Dahlonega–site of America's first gold rush

G. Okefenokee Swamp

H. Cumberland Island

I. Candy-cane striped Lighthouse on Sapelo Island

J. The Haunted Decatur Court House

K. Appalachian Trail

ANSWERS: 1-C; 2-A; 3-I; 4-J; 5-G; 6-B; 7-K; 8-D; 9-H; 10-E; 11-F

Make an Indian Vest!

Early Indians in Georgia wore clothing made from the skins of deer.

To make your deerskin vest, you will need a brown paper bag. Lay the bag flat as shown in the picture. Cut out holes for your arms and neck. Make a long slit in one side of the bag.

Ideas for decorating your vest:
- glue buttons, glitter, and feathers on the vest

- use markers or crayons to draw Indian symbols on the vest

- make fringe at the bottom of the bag by snipping along the edges of the bag

You can wear necklaces made of beads and shells to go with your vest.

Get together with your friends and have a great "pow-wow!"

Animal Scramble

**Unscramble the names of these animals you might find
in your Georgia backyard.**

Write the answers in the word wheel below the picture of each animal.

1. ***kipchnum***   Hint: She can store more than a hundred seeds in her cheeks!

2. ***ethiw dleait ered***   Hint: He raises the underside of his tail to signal danger!

3. ***nrocoac***   Hint: He has very sensitive "fingers" and uses them to find food.

4. ***ntseare ttoncoliat bitbra***   Hint: She would love to eat the cabbages in your garden!

5. ***yarg lquiersr***   Hint: He scurries around all day, burying and digging up acorns!

How Many People in Georgia?

CENSUS REPORT

Every ten years, it's time for Georgians to stand up and be counted. Since 1790, the United States has conducted a **census**, or count, of each of its citizens. Practice filling out a pretend census form.

Name _____ Age ☐

Place of Birth _____

Current Address _____

Does your family own or rent where you live? _____

How long have you lived in Georgia? _____

How many people are in your family? _____

How many females? ☐   How many males? ☐

What are their ages? _____

How many rooms are in your house? ☐

How is your home heated? _____

How many cars does your family own? ☐

How many telephones in your home? ☐

Is your home a farm? _____

Sounds pretty nosy, doesn't it? But a census is very important. The information is used for all kinds of purposes, including setting budgets, zoning land, determining how many schools to build, and much more. The census helps Georgia leaders plan for the future needs of its citizens. Hey, that's you!!

It's Still The Real Thing!

Coca-Cola is the "Unofficial" State Beverage of Georgia. It was invented in 1886 as a headache remedy by pharmacist John S. Pemberton. First year sales averaged 13 drinks a day at Jacob's Pharmacy in Atlanta where it was introduced. Today, Coca-Cola earns more than $13 billion in sales and holds four of the top five spots for best-selling soft drinks.

Coca-Cola has 15 top secret ingredients and is sold in 160 nations worldwide!

WOW! A soft drink that's been around the world and back again!

If ALL of these glasses of soda are half full, how many full glasses would you have if you added them together?

IS THIS GLASS HALF FULL OR HALF EMPTY?

You can find out everything you ever wanted to know about Coke at the World of Coca-Cola in Atlanta. You even get free samples!

ANSWERS: 5

How Does Your Garden Grow?

Since Georgia settlers didn't have super-big, super-new grocery stores to visit to do their grocery shopping, gardens were very important to them.

Can you "dig out" or "uproot" the fruits and veggies grown in this story?

There are 22 vegetables or fruits named here.

Can you find all of them? Write the names on the lines below.

Never disparage the asparagus! Chase the scarlet runner bean! You can't beat a beet! Do you see the broccoli? Let's lumber along the cucumber. Is that a chicken in the eggplant? Here's the beginning of the endive. I give a fig for figs! Salute the London flag leek! Toss some tennis ball lettuce in the net! Are you feeling melon, cauliflower? Oh, for some okra! Walk like an Egyptian onion! May I have some May peas, please? Bully for the bullnose pepper! Cheesecake pumpkin must make good pie! The ravishing red radish is blushing! The yellow crookneck squash has warts! The very merry strawberry is giggling. A Spanish tomato is red as a cape!

_____ _____

_____ _____

_____ _____

_____ _____

_____ _____

_____ _____

_____ _____

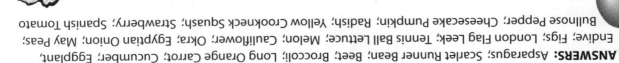

ANSWERS: Asparagus; Scarlet Runner Bean; Beet; Broccoli; Long Orange Carrot; Cucumber; Eggplant; Endive; Figs; London Flag Leek; Tennis Ball Lettuce; Melon; Cauliflower; Okra; Egyptian Onion; May Peas; Bullnose Pepper; Cheesecake Pumpkin; Radish; Yellow Crookneck Squash; Strawberry; Spanish Tomato

Colonial Corn Husk Doll

You can make a corn husk doll similar to the dolls Georgia settlers' children played with! Here's how:

You will need:
- corn husks (or strips of cloth)
- string
- scissors

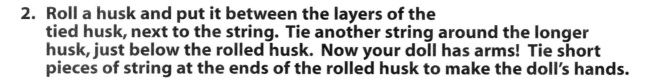

1. Select a long piece of corn husk and fold it in half. Tie a string about one inch down from the fold to make the doll's head.

2. Roll a husk and put it between the layers of the tied husk, next to the string. Tie another string around the longer husk, just below the rolled husk. Now your doll has arms! Tie short pieces of string at the ends of the rolled husk to make the doll's hands.

3. Make your doll's waist by tying another string around the longer husk.

4. If you want your doll to have legs, cut the longer husk up the middle. Tie the two halves at the bottom to make feet.

5. Add eyes and a nose to your doll with a marker. You could use corn silk for the doll's hair.

Now you can make a whole family of dolls!

The Scenic Route

Imagine that you are the official tour guide for your class and you're taking them on a trip to some famous Georgia places. *Watch out for that giant peach, James!*

Circle these sites and cities on the map below, then number them in the order you would visit if you were traveling north to south through the state:

____ Valdosta   ____ Atlanta   ____ Roswell   ____ Blue Ridge Mts.

____ Macon   ____ Plains   ____ Tifton   ____
Okefenokee Swamp

GEORGIA'S ALWAYS ON MY MIND!

How 'bout them Braves!

In 1966, the Milwaukee Braves moved to Atlanta. In 1975, media mogul and sports team owner, Ted Turner, purchased the baseball club. Two years later, during a long losing streak, he thought he'd try managing the club. Ted's managing days were short lived.

In 1991, with Manager Bobby Cox, the Braves went from worst in their division to first! Their winning ways continued and in 1995, the Atlanta Braves won the World Series!

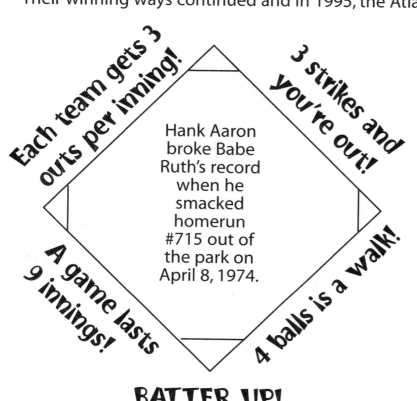

Each team gets 3 outs per inning!

3 strikes and you're out!

Hank Aaron broke Babe Ruth's record when he smacked homerun #715 out of the park on April 8, 1974.

A game lasts 9 innings!

4 balls is a walk!

BATTER UP!

Baseball Greats from Georgia include Ty Cobb–The Georgia Peach, and Jackie Robinson–the first African-American player in the National Baseball League!

The Atlanta Braves won the division title every year from 1991 through 1999.

Can you figure out how many division titles the Braves won in the 1990s?

The answer is _____.

Take me out to the ball game. Take me out to the crowd!

Buy me some peanuts and Cracker Jack. I don't care if I never get back!

ANSWER: 9

A Whale of a Tale!

The Right Whale, *Eubalaena glacialis*, is the State Marine Animal of Georgia. It is bluish-black with a lighter area on its belly. It has a stout body, a very large head, two blowholes, and no dorsal fin. These whales were considered "right" for hunting—that's where the name comes from! During the 1800s, they were nearly hunted to extinction, and remain rare today.

Now, see if you can answer the questions below.
Then, color the mother whale and her calf.

1. These are __ __ __ __ __ Whales.

2. Their *Latin* (or scientific) name is __ __ __ __ __ __ __ __ __ __ __ __ __ __ __ __ __ __ __ __ __ __ __ __.

3. Right Whales have __ __ __ blowholes, but they have no __ __ __ __ __ __ __ __fins!

4. Their color is bluish-black with a lighter area on their
   __ __ __ __ __ __ __ __.

5. Their bodies are __ __ __ __ __ and their heads are very __ __ __ __ __ __.

Please Come to Georgia!

You have a friend who lives in Arkansas. She is thinking of moving to Georgia because she has heard that there is a lot of economic development in the northeast megalopolis. You want to encourage your friend to come to Georgia.

Write her a letter describing Georgia and some of the employment opportunities.

_____
_____
_____
_____
_____
_____
_____
_____
_____
_____
_____
_____
_____
_____
_____
_____
_____
_____
_____
_____
_____
_____
_____
_____

Georgia is sometimes referred to as The Empire State of the South because of its thriving industry and size. Georgia is the largest state east of the Mississippi River!

Metropolitan Atlanta reaches out to include seven counties: Fulton, DeKalb, Cobb, Gwinnett, Clayton, Fayette, and Douglas.

GEORGIA IMMIGRATION

People have come to Georgia from other states and many other countries on almost every continent! As time has gone by, Georgia's population has grown more diverse. This means that people of different races and from different cultures and ethnic backgrounds have moved to Georgia.

In the past, many immigrants came to Georgia from Spain, England, Austria, Germany, Scotland, Wales, Italy, Switzerland, and other European countries. Slaves migrated (involuntarily) from Africa. More recently, people have migrated to Georgia from South American and Asian countries. Only a certain number of immigrants are allowed to move to America each year. Many of these immigrants eventually become U.S. citizens.

Read the statement and decide if it's fact or opinion.
Write your answer in the box.

1. Many of Georgia's early immigrants came from Europe.

2. Lots of immigrants speak a language other than English.

3. The clothing immigrants wear is very interesting.

4. Immigrants from England have a neat accent when they speak.

5. Many immigrants will become United States citizens.

6. Immigrants love Georgia's southern cooking.

7. Many recent immigrants come from South America and Asia.

An immigrant is a person who migrates to another country in hopes of a better life.

ANSWERS: 1-Fact; 2-Fact; 3-Opinion; 4-Opinion; 5-Fact; 6-Opinion; 7-Fact;

GEORGIA WOMEN AND THE VOTE!

In 1919, Georgia became the first state to reject the 19th Amendment to the United States Constitution giving women the right to vote. But in 1920, enough states ratified the amendment and it became the law of the land. Women gained suffrage nationally and began voting in Georgia for the first time. Women today continue to be a major force in the election process.

MORE TO LEARN:

Write the number of the phrase in column B that describes who or what each is in column A.

A

_____ Amendment

_____ Ratify

_____ Constitution

_____ General Assembly

_____ Law of the Land

_____ Election

_____ Suffrage

_____ Women

B

1. The right to vote

2. A law that is an acceptable practice throughout the nation

3. People who could not vote in Georgia until 1920

4. An addition to the Constitution

5. The selection, by vote, of a candidate for office

6. To give approval

7. The fundamental law of the United States that was framed in 1787 and put into effect in 1789

8. The legislature in some states of the United States

ANSWERS: 4-Amendment; 6-Ratify; 7-Constitution; 8-General Assembly; 2-Law of the Land; 5-Election; 1-Suffrage; 3-Women

GEORGIA SPELLING BEE

Good spelling is a good habit. It takes practice and will help you while you're in school and even while you're not!

Study the words on the left side of the page. Then fold the page in half and "take the spelling test" on the right side. Have a buddy read the words aloud to you. When done, unfold the page and check your spelling. Keep your score. GOOD LUCK.

Appalachian	1. _____
Brasstown Bald	2. _____
Chattahoochee	3. _____
Cherokee	4. _____
Emancipation	5. _____
Hartsfield	6. _____
Kennesaw	7. _____
Mound	8. _____
Nacoochee	9. _____
Oglethorpe	10. _____
Piedmont	11. _____
Sautee	12. _____
Savannah	13. _____
Vidalia	14. _____
Zoo Atlanta	15. _____

Each spelling word is worth 5 points. 75 is a perfect score. How many did you get right?

MY SCORE _____

Virtual Georgia!

Using your knowledge of Georgia, make a website that explains different places in the state. You can even draw pictures of animals, places, or people to make your very own website *very interesting*.

Home Sweet Home

Match these famous Georgia authors with their native or adopted hometowns. Atlanta, a very big and busy city, will be listed more than once!

A = Atlanta; B = Moreland; C = Eatonton; D = Columbus; E = Savannah; F = Macon; G = Fayetteville

_____	1.	**Margaret Mitchell:** novelist who wrote *Gone With the Wind.*
_____	2.	**Sidney Lanier:** poet who wrote *Marshes of Glynn* and *Song of the Chattahoochee.*
_____	3.	**Joel Chandler Harris (Uncle Remus):** novelist who wrote *Uncle Remus, His Songs and Sayings, Nights with Uncle Remus,* and *Uncle Remus and His Friends.*
_____	4.	**Alice Walker:** Pulitzer Prize winning novelist, poet, and writer of short stories, who wrote *The Color Purple.*
_____	5.	**Lewis Grizzard:** columnist and novelist who wrote *Daddy was a Pistol* and *I'm a Son of a Gun.*
_____	6.	**Alfred Uhry:** Pulitzer Prize winning playwright who wrote *Driving Miss Daisy.*
_____	7.	**Carson Smith McCullers:** novelist who wrote *The Heart Is a Lonely Hunter and Clock Without Hands.*
_____	8.	**Ferrol Sams:** physician and novelist who wrote *Run With the Horseman.*
_____	9.	**James Dickey:** novelist and poet who wrote *Deliverance* and *Buckdancer's Choice*
_____	10.	**Mary Flannery O'Connor:** novelist and writer of short stories; wrote *Wise Blood* and *Everything That Rises Must Converge*

ANSWERS: 1-A; 2-F; 3-C; 4-C; 5-B; 6-A; 7-D; 8-G; 9-A; 10-E

Let's Make Words—
Lots and Lots of Words!

Make as many words as you can from the letters in

Georgia, the Peach State

_____   _____   _____

_____   _____   _____

_____   _____   _____

_____   _____   _____

_____   _____   _____

_____   _____   _____

_____   _____   _____

_____   _____   _____

_____   _____   _____

_____   _____   _____

_____   _____   _____

_____   _____   _____

The Cherokee People

The Cherokees had a well established culture in north Georgia with an organized government similar to the United States. They spoke the Iroquoian language and were generally considered a peace-loving people. They were the largest of the civilized tribes in the Southeast. Their capital city was New Echota.

Sequoyah was a Cherokee silversmith, warrior, trader, and scholar. In 1821, he invented a written alphabet based on the sounds of his native language.

Sequoyah devoted his life to helping his people!

Sequoyah's alphabet, the first of its kind for Native Americans, enabled the Cherokee to read and write in their own language. His alphabet was used to record Cherokee history and publish newspapers and books.

Beginning with the first letter, select every other bubble to discover the name of the bilingual (two language) Cherokee newspaper that began publication in 1828.

1828 turned out to be a very bad year for the Cherokee people in northern Georgia. During that year, gold was discovered on their land, near the city of Dahlonega. Over the next ten years, their laws were declared null and void (that means they don't have any value or exist anymore). Their lands were taken away from them and they were forced to sign the Treaty of New Echota.

In 1838, under the terms of the treaty, the United States Army forced more than 15,000 Cherokee to leave their homes and undertake a grueling march to a reservation in Oklahoma. Those who would not leave were executed. More than 4,000 died on the way. The Cherokee who survived the journey from their homeland called it "The Trail Where They Cried" or "The Trail of Tears."

ANSWER: *The Cherokee Phoenix*

This Old House!

Take yourself back 100 years. Can you imagine what life would be like in the Victorian Era? What did turn-of-the-century Georgians have? How did they live? See if you can pick out which of the following items people at the turn of the century used in their homes!

Circle the things you find or use around your 1900 home.

1.
3.
5.
6.
7.
8.
2.
4.
9.
10.
11.
12.
13.
15.
14.
16.
17.
18.
19.
20.
21.
22.

Georgia
People

A state is not just towns and mountains and rivers. A state is its people! Lots of important people in a state may be famous, but lots of them may not be. They may be your mom, your dad, or your teacher. The average, everyday person helps make the state a good place to live. How? By working hard, by paying taxes, by voting, and by helping Georgia children grow up to be good state citizens!

Match each Georgia person with their accomplishment.

1. Jimmy Carter
2. Dr. Martin Luther King, Jr.
3. Ray Charles
4. Ty Cobb
5. Oliver Hardy
6. Trisha Yearwood
7. Jackie Robinson
8. Henry W. Grady
9. Walt Kelly
10. Crawford W. Long
11. Eli Whitney
12. Samuel L. Jackson
13. Juliette Gordon Low
14. Rebecca Latimer Felton
15. John Ross

A. Surgeon–first to use ether as anesthesia
B. Comedian–Laurel and Hardy
C. 39th U.S. President
D. Journalist and editor
E. Actor
F. Professional baseball player
G. Clergyman, civil rights leader
H. Founder of the Girl Scouts
I. Country singer
J. Pianist, song writer, and singer
K. Professional baseball player
L. Cartoonist, creator of "Pogo"
M. Inventor of the Cotton Gin–helped make cotton "King" in the South
N. First female United States senator
O. Cherokee Chief

ANSWERS: 1-C; 2-G; 3-J; 4-F; 5-B; 6-I; 7-K; 8-D; 9-L; 10-A; 11-M; 12-E; 13-H; 14-N; 15-O

Georgia Gazetteer

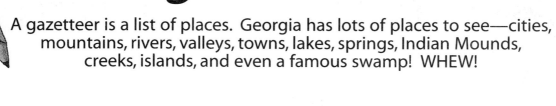

A gazetteer is a list of places. Georgia has lots of places to see—cities, mountains, rivers, valleys, towns, lakes, springs, Indian Mounds, creeks, islands, and even a famous swamp! WHEW!

Use the word bank to complete the names of some of these famous places in Georgia:

1. _ _ _ s s _ _ _ n Bald Mountain

2. _ h _ t t _ h _ _ _ h _ _ River

3. _ k _ f _ _ _ k _ _ Swamp

4. _ _ g _ l _ _ River

5. The city of _ _ p _ _ _ l _ k _ _

6. Lake _ _ n _ _ r

7. The capital city of _ t _ _ _ t _

8. _ h _ _ k _ _ _ _ l Mountain

9. Black Rock Mountain _ t _ t _ _ _ _ k

10. _ h _ k _ _ _ _ g _ Creek

11. J _ _ _ _ r _ Springs

12. The city of _ _ l _ _ _ _ _ _ r _ _ h

13. K _ _ _ _ _ _ k _ Mounds

14. _ _ c _ _ c h _ _ Valley

15. T _ b _ _ Island

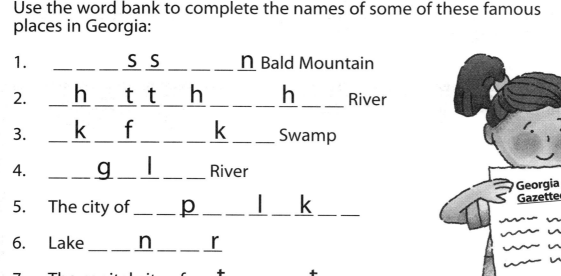

WORD BANK

- State Park
- Nacoochee
- Kolomoki
- Tybee

- Atlanta
- Chickamauga
- Jay Bird
- Chattahoochee
- Flowery Branch
- Brasstown
- Tugaloo

- Lanier
- Chunky Gal
- Okefenokee
- Hopeulikit

YOU'VE GOT MAIL!

CLICK ON THE ABSURD!

Send an e-mail to the past. E-mail a boy or girl from early Georgia and tell them what they're missing in today's world.

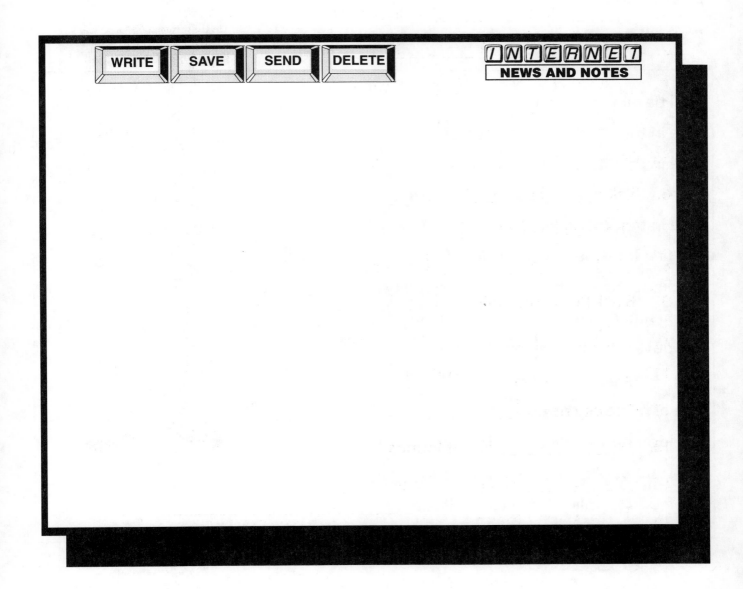

| WRITE | SAVE | SEND | DELETE |

INTERNET
NEWS AND NOTES

And who knows. You may even get a message in return…a message written on parchment with a quill pen telling you what you're missing from a simpler time!

Getting Ready To Vote

When you turn 18, you will eligible to vote. Your vote counts! Many elections have been won by just a few votes.

The following is a form for your personal voting information.

You will need to do some research to get all the answers!

I will be eligible to vote on this date _____

I live in this Congressional District _____

I live in this State Senate District _____

I live in this State Representative District _____

I live in this Voting Precinct _____

The first local election I can vote in will be _____

The first state election I can vote in will be _____

The first national election I can vote in will be _____

The governor of our state is _____

One of my state senators is _____

One of my state representatives is _____

The local public office I would like to run for is _____

The state public office I would like to run for is _____

The federal public office I would like to run for is _____

Ballot Box

Georgia Law Comes In Many Flavors!

Here is a matching activity for you to see just a few of the many kinds of law it takes to run our state. See how well you do!

If I am this, I might use what type of law?

1. Bank robber
2. Business person
3. State park
4. Georgia
5. Hospital
6. Real estate agent
7. Corporation
8. Ship owner
9. Diplomat
10. Soldier

Laws of many types:

A. Military Law
B. International Law
C. Constitutional Law
D. Medical Law
E. Maritime Law
F. Commercial Law
G. Criminal Law
H. Property Law
I. Antitrust Law
J. Environmental Law

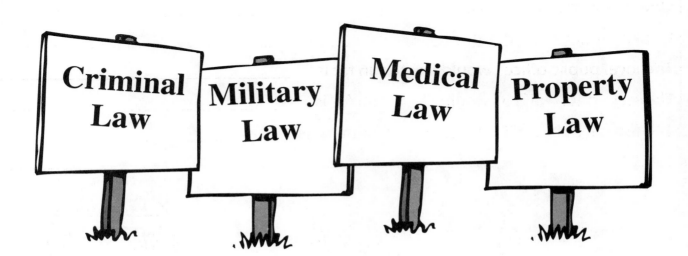

ANSWERS: 1-G; 2-F; 3-J; 4-C; 5-D; 6-H; 7-I; 8-E; 9-B; 10-A

Design your own Diamante on Georgia!

A *diamante* is a cool diamond-shaped poem on any subject.

You can write your very own diamante poem on Georgia by following the simple line by line directions below. Give it a try!

Line 1: Write the name of your state

Line 2: Write the name of two animals native to your state

Line 3: Write the names of three of your state's important cities

Line 4: Write the name of four of your state's important industries or agricultural products.

Line 5: Write the names of your state bird, the state flower, and state tree

Line 6: Write the name of two of your state's geographical features

Line 7: Write the name of your state's nickname

_____

_____ _____

_____ _____ _____

_____ _____ _____ _____

_____ _____ _____

_____ _____

_____

James Dickey was the "unofficial" Poet Laureate during Jimmy Carter's Administration. He read his poem "The Strength of Fields" at the pre-inaugural gala.

David Bottoms, a professor at Georgia State University, is Georgia's Poet Laureate.

"I Have a Dream..."

Georgians were very involved in the civil rights movement of America. Dr. Martin Luther King, Jr. had a dream that all Americans would be treated equally and he worked hard to make that dream come true! In March 1960, Dr. King supported students at Atlanta University when they published "An Appeal for Human Rights" in the Atlanta daily papers. The document stated their intentions to secure full citizenship rights for African-Americans through nonviolent demonstrations and legal actions. In 1961, schools in Atlanta and Athens began to abandon their policy of segregation. Other cities in Georgia followed close behind!

Many other African-Americans from Georgia made significant contributions to the state, the nation, and in some cases, the world!

Fill in the blanks with the name of these Georgians who played an important role in the civil rights movement!

1. In 1962, __ __ __ __ __ __ __ __ __ __ __ __ __ became the first African-American elected to Georgia's State Senate.

2. __ __ __ __ __ __ __ __ __ __ __ __ __ __ __ __ __ was the first African-American to hold the position of mayor of Atlanta.

3. __ __ __ __ __ __ __ __ __ __ __ __ __ __ __ __ __ __ __ __ __ __ served as director of the Southern Christian Leadership Conference. He was elected to the U.S. Congress. President Jimmy Carter appointed him U.S. Ambassador to the United Nations, and he later served as mayor of Atlanta for two terms.

4. __ __ __ __ __ __ __ __ __ __ served in the Georgia House of Representatives.

5. Mrs. __ __ __ __ __ __ __ __ __ __ __ __ __ __ __ __ __ __ continues the work her husband, Dr. Martin Luther King, Jr., began.

6. __ __ __ __ __ __ __ __ __ __ __ __ __ __ __ __ __ __ __ __ __ __ __ was an author and civil rights leader. He served as secretary of the National Association for the Advancement of Colored People.

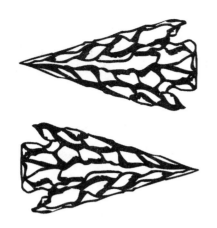

Georgia Wheel of Fortune, Indian Style!

The names of Georgia's many Native American Indian tribes contain enough letters to play ... Wheel of Fortune!

See if you can figure out the Wheel of Fortune-style puzzles below! "Vanna" has given you the consonants in each word to help you out!

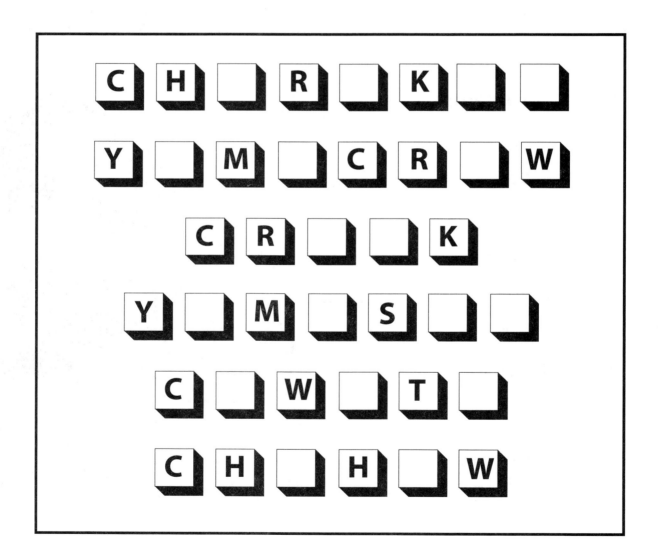

C H □ R R K □ □

Y □ M □ C R □ W

C R □ □ K

Y □ M □ S □ □

C □ W □ T □

C H □ H □ W

BROTHER, CAN YOU SPARE A DIME?

After the collapse of the stock market on Wall Street in 1929, the state of Georgia, along with the rest of the nation, fell into the Great Depression. It was the worst economic crisis America had ever known. Many banks closed and many businesses failed.

Our President Helps.
During the Depression, Franklin Delano Roosevelt became president of the United States. The federal government tried to help American families by hiring unemployed people to work on federal building projects. Through these programs and other government assistance, the country began to slowly pull out of the Great Depression. Within the first 100 days of his office, President Roosevelt enacted a number of policies to ease the suffering of the nation's many unemployed workers. These programs were known as the NEW DEAL. The jobs helped families support themselves and made many improvements to our nation's parks, bridges, and roads.

Put an X next to the jobs that were part of Roosevelt's New Deal

1. computer programmer _____

2. bridge builder _____

3. fashion model _____

4. park builder _____

5. interior designer _____

6. hospital builder _____

7. school builder _____

8. web site designer _____

9. road builder _____

President Franklin D. Roosevelt built his Little White House in Warm Springs, Georgia.

ANSWERS: 2; 4; 6; 7; 9

IT'S MONEY IN THE BANK!!

You spent the summer working at your uncle's manufacturing plant in Peachtree City and you made a lot of money...$500 to be exact! Decide how you will spend it below.

TOTAL EARNED:	$500.00

I will pay back my Mom this much for money I borrowed when I first started working (Thanks Mom!):   A. $20.00

Subtract A ($20.00) from $500   B. _____

I will give my little brother this much money for taking my phone messages while I was at work: C. $10.00

Subtract C ($10.00) from B   D. _____

I will spend this much on a special treat or reward for myself: E. $25.00

Subtract E ($25.00) from D   F. _____

   G. $300.00

I will save this much for college:

Subtract G ($300.00) from F   H. _____

I will put this much in my new savings account so I can buy school clothes: I. $100.00

Subtract I ($100.00) from H   J. _____

TOTAL STILL AVAILABLE
(use answer J)   _____

TOTAL SPENT
(add A, C, and E)   _____

ANSWERS: B-$480.00; D-$470.00; F-$445.00; H-$145.00; J-$45.00; TOTAL SPENT: $55.00

A SHORT AND SWEET HISTORY OF OUR STATE WITH YOU AS THE AUTHOR

Make your own timeline, based on research, for the following major events in the history of Georgia. Use an encyclopedia, almanac, or any other resource you feel is appropriate! We will give you the time period...you pick a major event that happened!

Early exploration   _____

Early settlement   _____

American Revolution   _____

Colonial era   _____

Slavery era   _____

Civil War   _____

Immigrants arrive   _____

Great Depression   _____

World War I   _____

Korean War   _____

World War II   _____

Vietnam War   _____

Civil Rights era   _____

Information Age   _____

Frontier Era   _____

Come and Find Me!

Time for a scavenger hunt! Can you dig around and find the answers for the following questions? Good luck!

On your mark, get set, get ready, *GO!*

1 In the beginning, an English ship came to Savannah and brought James Oglethorpe and English settlers to Georgia. Write the name of the boat here __ __ __ __ __ __ __.

2. The __ __ __ __ __ __ __ __ __ __ __ __ __ won the 1995 World Series.

3. What are the Georgia 3 P's and a V? __ __ __ __ __ __ __ , __ __ __ __ __ __ __ , __ __ __ __ __ __ , and __ __ __ __ __ __ __ onions.

4. The Summer Olympics were held in Atlanta in what year? Write your answer here: _____.

5. The Okefenokee Swamp has _____ alligators that live there.

6. Jimmy Carter was the _____ President of the United States.

7. You can vote in Georgia when you're _____ years old!

8. Dr. Martin Luther King, Jr. was very involved in America's __ __ __ __ __ __ __ __ __ __ __ movement.